The life of Bellini

Musical lives

The books in this series will each provide an account of the life of a major composer, considering both the private and the public figure. The main thread will be biographical and discussion of the music will be integral to the narrative. Each book thus presents an 'organic' view of the composer, the music, and the circumstances in which he or she lived and wrote.

The life of Bellini

JOHN ROSSELLI

CAMBRIDGE
UNIVERSITY PRESS

Published by the Press Syndicate of the University of Cambridge
The Pitt Building, Trumpington Street, Cambridge CB2 1RP
40 West 20th Street, New York, NY 10011–4211, USA
10 Stamford Road, Oakleigh, Melbourne 3166, Australia

First published 1996

Printed in Great Britain at the University Press, Cambridge

A catalogue record for this book is available from the British Library

Library of Congress cataloguing in publication data

Rosselli, John.
    The life of Bellini / John Rosselli.
        p.   cm. – (Musical lives)
    Includes discography, bibliographical references, and index.
        ISBN 0 521 46227 4 (hardback). ISBN 0 521 46781 0 (paperback)
        1. Bellini, Vincenzo, 1801–1835.   2. Composers – Italy – Biography.
    I. Title.   II. Series.
    ML410.B44R77   1996
    782.1′092–dc20   95–39270   CIP   MN
    [B]

ISBN 0 521 46227 4 hardback
ISBN 0 521 46781 0 paperback

SE

CONTENTS

This book sets out to provide a short critical biography of Bellini, seen in his historical context. Most of it rests on a fresh examination of published sources. The one matter on which I have done a good deal of new archival research is the identity of three people Bellini associated with in Paris; so as not to clutter up the narrative, this is dealt with in the Appendix. I have also drawn on my earlier research into the Italian opera industry and the singing profession.

Such a book would not normally call for much if any annotation, apart from the Appendix, where new matter, potentially controversial, demands precise references. As the Introduction explains, however, the published evidence for Bellini's career is flawed and some is faked. This is the first book to challenge it radically – though only by applying the normal methods of historical criticism. Where I deny or cast doubt on the validity of supposed documents I need to give evidence and reasons. This has meant some (at times long) notes, which readers may choose to take in or not.

Quotations from Bellini's letters are generally followed by the date(s) of the letter(s) in brackets. This makes it possible to follow up the sources in the collections listed in the Note on further reading; nearly all are in Bellini's *Epistolario*, ed. L. Cambi, Milan, 1943.

I have been considerably and kindly helped with information and documentation by Lorenzo Bianconi, Peter Day, Salvatore Enrico Failla, Simon Maguire, Pierluigi Petrobelli, and Alessandro Roccatagliati. My thanks to all of them, and to the librarians of the Bibliothèque de l'Opéra, Paris, and the Library of Performing Arts, New York.

Introduction: rediscovering Bellini

Bellini keeps being rediscovered. For more than a hundred years he has at intervals seemed eclipsed. Then something happens: Rosa Ponselle or Maria Callas sings Norma; *La sonnambula* or *I puritani* – each, one might have thought, a quintessential early Victorian work – comes up fresh in a new staging; taste shifts away from the full-blown and towards the linear. Bellini then springs to life as a unique artist.

One rediscovery came in the 1920s, another in the 1950s. One more is probably due now, though modern recording keeps the three operas just named in the public ear as essential to the repertory even when, with Callas dead and other virtuosos in retirement, they are seldom staged. Records also bring forward works long forgotten – *Il pirata, La straniera*, the un-Shakespearian Romeo and Juliet opera *I Capuleti e i Montecchi*, even *Zaira*, the failure Bellini in part recycled as *Capuleti*. The Italian public has never forsaken Bellini, even when – between about 1890 and 1920 – the intelligentsia dismissed him; today his portrait is on the 5,000-lira note. Discriminating music-lovers elsewhere should agree that he is a highly individual composer, major in stature though his output is small and in effect limited to opera.

Bellini is a major composer as Andrew Marvell is a major poet. No one could sensibly call the author of 'The Garden', 'To his Coy Mistress', and the Horatian Ode a minor poet: his voice is original, his grasp masterly; phrase after phrase has taken root in the minds of

1 Continuing fame: the head of Bellini on the Italian 5,000-lira note, current in
1995.

the literate. Marvell wrote little because he was a busy parliamentari-
an and fastidious. Bellini wrote little because he died at thirty-three;
once out of music school he wrote operas because opera was the
genre open to an ambitious young Italian, and by the standards of
the time he too was fastidious, composing on average one opera a
year where others composed three or four. 'With my style', he wrote,
'I have to spit blood [to compose]' (14 June 1828). People in his day
drew a parallel with his close contemporary Chopin, another elegiac
composer unique in his genre. The likeness can still at times seem
uncanny, though any influence was marginal (of Bellini on the
younger Chopin rather than the other way about) and the 'elegiac'
label was always overdone: Bellini, like Chopin, could be forceful.

His work has often been called uneven. This is true: *Norma* itself,
his masterpiece, has lapses; only *La sonnambula* keeps up an even quality – in a medium (the idyll) not now fashionable. 'The poet's privilege', Bernard Shaw wrote, is to have 'his chain tested by its strongest
link'. The composer's too. Bellini's strongest links are adamant.

To the biographer he sets a problem. He died young, at the height
both of his success and of the Romantic movement; he was not only

good-looking but fair-haired and blue-eyed – a fair-haired, blue-eyed Sicilian at that. For all these reasons he became an instant myth. The wan, baseless legend then promoted ('a sigh in dancing pumps', Heine called him) dragged on through the rest of the century and beyond.

The myth took hold not just of the public at large but of Bellini's intimate friend Francesco Florimo, who tended his memory and, much later (1882), brought out an early biography. In twice-weekly letters to him Bellini had shared his professional concerns, his most private thoughts and feelings, almost his stream of consciousness. Florimo's treatment of those letters through five decades of living with the myth badly complicates our understanding. Other friends, and some later editors, played their part in muddying the evidence. A biographer has to be a detective.

The circumstances of Bellini's death had much to do with starting up the myth. He died on 23 September 1835 at a friend's rented house in the suburban village of Puteaux, just outside Paris. His illness, recurring dysentery caused by amoebic infection, had not been properly diagnosed and was anyhow incurable by the medicine of the time. He had fallen ill in late summer when many of his acquaintances were away from central Paris, as he was himself. Less than eight months had gone by since his great Parisian success with I puritani, only a few weeks since he had been in society, apparently healthy. For all these reasons his death came as a shock.

Early obituaries in French journals did not unanimously praise his music; but even their criticisms dwelt on the stereotype of the 'elegiac and tender' composer, author of 'slow and languid phrases'. Berlioz, with many reservations, praised his 'deep sensibility', 'melancholy grace', and 'naive simplicity' as a composer, his 'even temper' and 'pleasant demeanour' as a man. Articles and diaries called him a 'child' in his goodheartedness and his enthusiasms; some understated his age. At the same time they exaggerated his success in Paris society (Bellini had indeed been taken up in the salons, but, for reasons to be examined later, had found them

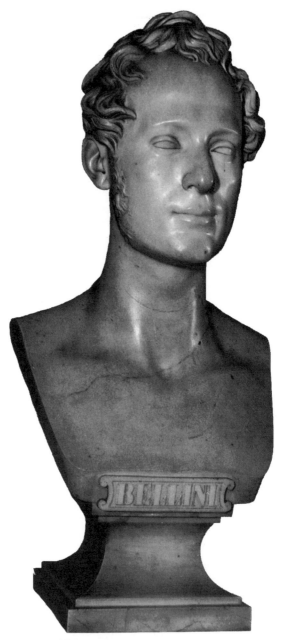

2 Marble bust of Bellini by Dantan Jeune, commissioned
by the sixth Duke of Devonshire.

baffling and had twice withdrawn to the calm of Puteaux). The worst anybody could say of him was that he had overdone the pursuit of pleasure.

By 1863 the myth was encapsulated in the reminiscences of the publisher Léon Escudier: the young Sicilian 'blond as the cornfields, sweet as the angels, young as the dawn, melancholy as the sunset. There was in his soul something of both Pergolesi and Mozart', etc. In the Romantic era numbers of artists died young (Chatterton, Keats, Shelley, and Byron among English poets). They fed a notion of doomed genius; in music doom could be read into the lives of Pergolesi and Mozart – each the subject of a considerable myth – and now into Bellini's.

In Naples, where Bellini had studied, ladies on the night of his requiem mass attended a performance of *Norma* in mourning. In his native Catania a flora of legends grew up about his precocious childhood and his alleged youthful love affairs; the earliest biographer with some pretensions picked up in 1855 stories of the eighteen-month-old Bellini 'gracefully' singing and transposing an aria. In Florence a collector of musicians' autographs had already (1849) cut a letter of Bellini's in pieces and sold them as relics. But the trigger to the most extravagant myth-making was the removal of Bellini's body from the Père-Lachaise cemetery in Paris to Catania Cathedral.

This happened in 1876. As the coffin made its way down the Italian peninsula it was met at station after station by bands, speeches, laurel crowns. In Catania, several days' processions, masses, illuminations, public meetings and concerts preceded the reburial; of the many speeches one, by a scientist, urged that the next star to be discovered should be named Bellini. Experts meanwhile re-embalmed the mummified corpse as it lay in a side-chapel of the cathedral. An American soprano, Mary Louise Swift, engaged to sing in a memorial cantata, talked her way into the chapel and begged to be allowed to kiss Bellini. As she did so she plucked two hairs from his chest. Nor was she alone in this. Through the good offices of the embalmers various people got hold of hairs, some from the head, some again from the chest; one hair became a string in a lyre embroidered by another woman admirer, while others found their way into a red velvet-covered box alongside a fragment of the original coffin, 'residual organic substances', and a trepan used in the re-embalming.

In this atmosphere it is hardly surprising that Bellini's great friend Francesco Florimo should have ignored scholarly methods in dealing with the composer's many letters to him. When Bellini left for Milan (1827) and then Paris (1833) Florimo stayed behind in Naples, wedded as librarian to the college they had both attended. He made it his life's work – through a long life – to propagate the cult both of Bellini and of the Neapolitan musical tradition his friend had adorned. Publications from 1869 culminated in *Bellini. Memorie e lettere* (1882), a biography followed by over 200 pages of letters. Florimo died six years later, bequeathing many autograph letters to the college library.

Bellini's letters to Florimo are still our chief evidence for his life, working methods, and personality. This evidence, however, is skewed. Those letters of which the originals can be consulted are an extraordinarily frank and detailed source – few artists have written down their every passing mood as Bellini did – but they cover only the periods from January 1828 to March 1829 and from July 1834 to September 1835, with a scattering of letters in between. Letters to other correspondents go some way to fill the gap of more than five years, but they are nowhere near so free.

What happened? Florimo burned many letters, clearly because they dated from the years when Bellini was having an affair with a married woman, Giuditta Turina; the affair ended in 1834, just after it had led to her separation from her husband, and a full knowledge of the circumstances might have shown the composer in an unflattering light. Florimo, however, went further. As he tells us, he gave away some letters to admirers who begged for a memento, and he did not keep copies; since there was a market in the letters, and at least one addressed to him turned up in the hands of an autograph dealer, we may ask whether he did not at times eke out his librarian's income by selling them. In his publications he also faked a number of letters or parts of letters.

'Fake' is a strong word. Writers on Bellini have so far avoided it; though aware that these letters are not in Bellini's style and are on other grounds dubious, they have concluded that Florimo (like some other nineteenth-century editors of dubious Bellini letters) must have worked them up from originals now lost, or from something Bellini had said in conversation. Passages from them have therefore remained central to interpretation.

In using the word I mean not just that Florimo behaved like the run of nineteenth-century editors, who corrected letters for grammar and style, tacitly bowdlerized them, and on occasion ran two letters together or split one letter into two. He did all these things, but he went further: he invented new matter that substantially changed the view of Bellini's feelings presented by his letters. He also recalled conversations some of which could not have taken place.

Of all the dubious published letters only two have an autograph original fully known to us. One of these autographs may be read in full, together with the letter as published by Florimo.[1] A comparison tells us much about his methods.

As a student in Naples Bellini was for a time in love with Maddalena Fumaroli, a judge's daughter, and she, for rather longer, with him. The story is known almost wholly from Florimo's narrative; it launched fanciful accounts by others, such as a play of 1878 that showed Giuditta Turina as villainess, and Bellini at Maddalena's deathbed. In reality, Bellini lost interest in Maddalena as soon as he left for Milan if not sooner; he found her letters irksome. She died in June 1834; it is not clear from Bellini's autograph letter of a year later whether he had only then heard of her death, or was recalling his feelings in answer to a question put by Florimo.

In the autograph Maddalena takes up fifteen lines partway through a letter of seventy-four. This is one topic among others: a rumoured duel, commissions and accounts, dealings with publishers and with a

Naples opera management, an importunate acquaintance. The letter
has two points in common with Florimo's published version:

1 Bellini 'wept bitterly' at the news, and realized that his heart
  was still 'capable of feeling sorrow' (though part of the point –
  unmentioned in Florimo's version – was to contrast this with
  his behaviour at parting from Giuditta Turina);

2 he asked for a poem to set to music as a memorial (requested
  by someone in Naples) and that it should have him addressing
  Maddalena's 'beautiful spirit'.

In Florimo's published version, however – entirely taken up with
Maddalena, – Bellini was also made to declare that

1 the news had 'broken his heart', produced a 'rending sensation' in
  his spirit, called up memories, promises, and hopes, and brought
  out the transitoriness of 'this world of vain shows';

2 he had tried to sing Florimo's memorial song 'between sobs', and
  his heart was 'wounded';

3 his pen, as he wrote, was falling from his hand and tears prevented
  him from going on;

4 Maddalena's death, a 'thunderbolt' that appeared to signal divine
  wrath, made him foresee his own.

This last, a substantial postscript two-thirds the length of the letter,
had no basis whatever in Bellini's autograph, but it came pat in a letter supposedly written three and half months before his death.

What are we to conclude? The first third of the letter in Florimo's
version is invented, the last sentence and the postscript are invented,
and the rest, though based on the autograph, has been worked up to
deepen the feeling and purge it of all mention of Bellini's physical
relationship with Turina. By the standards of everyday historical criticism, the whole is a fake, not just because Florimo has inserted so
much new matter but because he has isolated and blown up the topic
of Bellini's (genuine) sorrow at the young woman's death to give it
an importance the original letter does not convey.

That was a special case. The other fully documented example shows Florimo's everyday method. Bellini on 14 February 1834 answered a request from the management of the Teatro San Carlo, Naples, for a new opera. His autograph letter is sober and businesslike. Florimo's version (for which there exists a draft as well as the published text) does not change the basic meaning but seeks to make the letter more stylish and patriotic. Bellini's reference to 'the means' nature had granted him becomes 'those few means'; 'persons for whom I am to write' becomes 'persons to whom I was to entrust my [musical] notes'; operatic failures are additionally described as 'an illness that has now become an epidemic'. Bellini is made to express satisfaction at writing 'for the country that saw my birth and that trained me in my difficult art' and, later, at the chance of 'gathering glory on the soil of my beloved fatherland'. The letter is not altogether a fake, but it is distorted: the new version suggests a fatuous wish to impress that is nowhere to be seen in the original.[2]

Several other letters or fragments of letters published by Florimo are dubious. The original of one was sold at Sotheby's in 1990. In this letter (of 7 October 1834) Bellini urged his librettist Felice Romani, with whom he had been reconciled after a breach, to write 'for me only'; though Sotheby's catalogue quotes no more than extracts, we do now know that Florimo worked this up to 'for *me only: only for me, for your* Bellini' – a phrase quoted by every biographer – and, where the original was friendly but sober, added whole sentences extravagantly buttering up Romani: 'I will never be able to forget your aid and the glory that I owe to you', 'Now that we are reconciled, O my great Romani, my eminent collaborator and protector, I feel at peace and am content', 'I can't wait to embrace you.' Again Bellini's tone and attitude are falsified.

Another dubious letter has Bellini attending the first night of *La sonnambula* in London with the great Maria Malibran: he calls out 'brava!', is recognized, acclaimed, and dragged on to the stage to take a bow; Malibran flings her arms round him, singing the phrase he had applauded ('Ah! Embrace me!'). The text runs to fanciful journalese ('the blond sons of Albion') unlike Bellini's plain, at times clumsy epistolary style. If we look up reviews in the London *Morning Chronicle* and *Morning Herald* we find that they differ about the success of the performance – the less favourable one reports 'none of the music was encored', a statement of fact – but neither mentions Bellini's presence. Nor did Bellini, in an authentic letter to another friend, report any of the alleged incidents. Florimo's worked-up version seems aimed at confirming the story that Bellini had fallen in love with Malibran – a story popular almost since the death of both artists within a year of each other, but unlikely on several grounds; another 'fragment of a letter' published by Florimo jokes about a possible duel between Bellini and Malibran's lover (later her husband), but an authentic letter from Bellini to Malibran shows them on terms of mutual regard, at most exchanging a theatrical 'darling'.

Another celebrated letter, about the initial failure of *Norma* ('fiasco!!! fiasco!!! utter fiasco!!!') has generally been seen as not in Bellini's style, contradicted by authentic letters, and embellished at the least. Florimo declared that he had given the original to Sir William Temple, the British Minister at Naples (Lord Palmerston's brother), keeping, this time, a copy for himself. In her standard edition of the letters, Luisa Cambi argued that Florimo could not have made up the letter from start to finish for fear of contradiction by such important people as Temple and Palmerston. She was unaware that by 1868, when the letter first appeared, both were dead and the family was extinct.

Finally, Bellini's relations with his near-contemporary Donizetti called up a sustained endeavour by Florimo to show what we now know to be untrue – that the two composers had always lived in friendly harmony and mutual admiration. This was based on 'remembered conversations' and letters or letter 'fragments' for none of which are the originals known; both the memories and the letters throw up a number of internal contradictions.[3] Much if not all of this 'evidence' – we have to conclude – is faked.

Why did Florimo do it? We need not think him a conscious forger.

People treated him as, in effect, Bellini's widower. He and his friends for long dealt with Bellini's letters as relics to be prized and donated, like a saint's finger bone, not as documentation. After thirty or forty years of living – in Naples, a headquarters of fantasy – with the myth of a Bellini part doomed angel, part irresistible lover, he too identified Bellini with Pergolesi, and thought he remembered his friend saying that if he could write tender, passionate melodies like Pergolesi's he would be content to die just as young.

Florimo may at length have found it hard to tell truth from fiction. From the nineteenth-century editor's usual practice of correcting and censoring texts he may have slipped imperceptibly into making up what Bellini *must* have felt: who but he, Florimo, knew? Half-conscious myth-making might explain how he could assert that Bellini always admired and was on excellent terms with Donizetti, while he held in his files (and eventually bequeathed) authentic letters in which Bellini expressed deep suspicion and jealousy of the rival composer.

Nor was Florimo alone in making up evidence. Two Sicilians who had known Bellini published alleged letters that rang false: in one he grovelled to Rossini – unlike the complex relation to the older composer shown in his authentic letters; in another he set out his alleged working method, a method irreconcilable with his surviving sketches and his comments on them. As late as 1932 a biography published in Catania included new alleged letters, most of them love letters to or about various women, for none of which could the originals be found. This was too much: the 'letters' have been set aside by more respectable biographers. But they have still felt bound to print the earlier dubious letters and, often, to justify them as substantially correct.

This book departs from earlier practice and follows the historian's normal method. If a letter must reasonably be held false in whole or in part, the false statements will be ignored; if well known and oft-repeated, they will be briefly dismissed; if merely suspect, they will be mentioned with reservations.

A subtler danger is the total frankness of Bellini's authentic letters to Florimo, and the explicitness, almost as great, of some of the letters to his family in Catania.

These documents are, for a start, fragmentary. Even when there are enough to make up a sequence, we need to realize that the very fullness of what we have is uncommon. Not allowing for this led Herbert Weinstock in his 1971 biography to find Bellini 'in many ways unattractive', his letters at times 'unbalanced' and 'dangerously paranoid'.

Most adults have a wife, husband, or companion to whom they can blow off steam. They need not set down their passing doubts and resentments in letters for a biographer to dig up. Among Italian composers, Verdi could be harsh in his letters to fellow-members of the opera world, but he probably said far worse things in conversation with his wife. If we could eavesdrop on those conversations, we might think him 'dangerously paranoid'. Bellini had no one he could blow off steam to except correspondents far away; so he wrote it all down. He himself (as he told Florimo on 4 August 1834) was aware that his language when angry 'would not do me honour among people other than a constant and affectionate friend of fifteen years' standing such as you are'; he bade him repeat it 'to *no one!!!*' What if our stream of consciousness was similarly exposed?

We also need to see Bellini within his culture. His biographers have nearly all been people used to living by the word – even though they have been musicologists. The very length and tortuousness of many of Bellini's letters show that he was not a man of the word. His education and sensibility were in large part musical. Even his gift for word-setting in opera was an extension of his musical faculty.

He grew up on a remote island where most people spoke Sicilian in everyday life, and studied in a city where nearly everyone spoke Neapolitan. He then worked in northern Italy, where educated people often spoke dialects markedly unlike those of the south – in Milan interspersed with French. Finally, he lived in Paris, where he struggled with the language. What his spoken Sicilian or Neapolitan was like we do not know. His written Italian – at that time a literary and official language, and a lingua franca for the educated – was uncertain; like many people whose grasp of language is weak, he readily picked up foreign turns of phrase – Gallicisms – while failing to master the language they came from. All this calls for empathy and imagination as well as critical scrutiny.

Many artists' work seems to move on a plane other than that of their daily life. With Bellini the divergence is at first sight acute. He worked in the theatre, at most times a rough and tumble profession, in his day specially hurried and competitive. To the presentable it opened the doors of aristocratic society, to the gifted it offered the chance of wealth, but it kept nearly all its members to doubtful bohemian status and to the harsh discipline of the market. Verdi's wife, a famous singer in her youth, was to call it a 'stinking swamp'. That too was a bit of myth-making.

In studying Bellini's career we need to ask how the special purity of *La sonnambula* and *Norma* grew, not out of a swamp, but out of a busy world of new entertainments rapidly produced, in some ways akin to modern cinema or television. Within that world Bellini – a young southerner on the make – moved knowledgeably, imposed his own terms, and beat all his contemporaries to the top. His intimate sensibility, outwardly hidden from us, lies in his works. Such will be the guiding threads of this book.

1   A young southerner

As she delivered her first child Bellini's mother heard celestial music, and all the bells of Catania miraculously rang together. So said one of the legends popular in the city through the mid- and late nineteenth century. In his home town as elsewhere it was Bellini's early death that set off the myth. Contemporary evidence shows nothing special about his birth on 3 November 1801, his baptism next day (when, legend had it, Vincenzo was much moved at hearing his grandfather's music on the organ), his progress as a toddler (able at eighteen months, so a chronicle by an unnamed relative claimed much later, to sing a comic opera aria 'gracefully'), or his feats as a three-year-old (alleged by the same chronicler to have successfully beaten time from the score for a full orchestra). Like many musicians, Vincenzo was precocious, but not so strikingly as Mozart.

Catania in the first year of the century was a place fit for wonders. Etna's mighty cone loomed with its wisp of smoke above the city it had destroyed in 1693. Another eruption might come at any time; a serious earthquake was to come in 1818. Though its name went back to an ancient Greek settlement, Catania's fabric was newer than New York's was. It was still being rebuilt; baroque palaces and convents, their dark lava blocks trimmed with white stone carved into whorls and gargoyles, rose from streets themselves of lava, uneven as it had come to rest in 1693. All but five streets were unpaved; workshops lined them, pigs grouted amid the rubbish. Yet this was, for Sicily, a go-ahead place.

To modern ears Sicily calls up images all too familiar. The Mafia, though, did not exist in 1801; even when it began to take shape (about the time of Bellini's death) it did not for many years touch the east coast. Nor did Sicilians emigrate in numbers, save involuntarily when North African pirates caught them. The island was remote several times over. It lay on the edge of Europe, whose chief trade routes and manufacturing centres had long since shifted away from the Mediterranean and towards the north-west. Though a nominally independent kingdom, it had long had its king and central government elsewhere. After four centuries of Spanish rule, wars and treaties from 1713 to 1734 rapidly handed it to three other sovereigns in turn – those of Piedmont, then Austria, finally Naples – still as a nominally independent kingdom. Then, during the Napoleonic wars – in 1798–9, again in 1805–15 – it was cut off from a mainland dominated by the French; British ships and troops ensured that it did not then experience the administrative and social changes the French brought with them. Even after the fall of Napoleon brought back the old Italian monarchies (nine or ten, according to circumstance) under the general control of Austria, the island was still remote from most of them. Its largely agricultural economy depended on exports of wheat, then of sulphur; its small educated classes were just emerging from a cult of old-fashioned erudition and feudal law.

Yet 'Sicily' was something of an abstraction. With its three rival cities (Palermo, Messina, Catania) and its slow internal communications the island had no one focus. Unlike the swarming capital, Palermo – headquarters of a great nobility served by dependent craft guilds and backed by vast wheat-growing estates – Catania was a modest city of 45,000 people with a hinterland of vineyards and olive groves on rich volcanic soil. Its educated classes looked more to Naples – accessible by sea – and to the development of their port. When a political crisis in 1811–12 brought a new, short-lived parliamentary constitution a group of Catanese took the lead in preaching

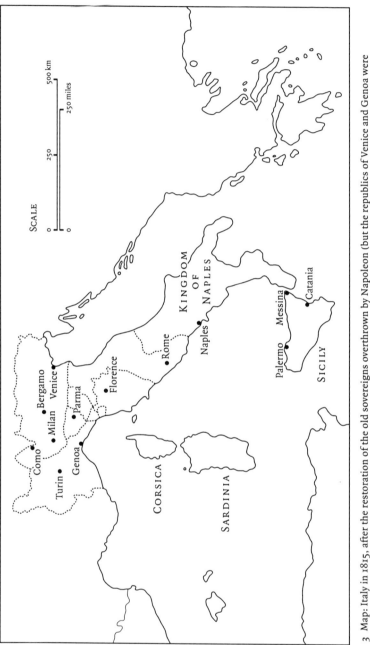

3 Map: Italy in 1815, after the restoration of the old sovereigns overthrown by Napoleon (but the republics of Venice and Genoa were absorbed, the one into the Austrian-ruled kingdom of Lombardy-Venetia, the other into the kingdom of Sardinia, ruled from Turin). In 1816 Sicily and Naples were united into the kingdom of the Two Sicilies, with its capital at Naples.

democracy. The end of the Napoleonic wars allowed the Bourbon king in 1816 to abolish the constitution and even the nominally independent Sicilian kingdom. Although this meant centralized despotism, it also meant a belated adoption of the modern, simplified administrative and judicial systems imposed elsewhere by Napoleon; Catania lawyers were quick to work them. Born as he was into a city dominated by this ambitious bourgeoisie – the leading historian Giuseppe Giarrizzo has argued – Bellini, though of humble origins, took easily to its 'high' culture and to a network of social relations that freed him from having to depend on patronage or nurse an inferiority complex; when the city corporation funded his musical schooling it sent him to like-minded Naples.

There is something in this; but the French Revolution, directly and indirectly, brought social changes such that nowhere in Europe could a leading musician any longer wear a nobleman's livery as Haydn had done down to 1790. Bourgeois dominance in Catania was relative – the work of lawyers and officials who were also minor landowners rather than of merchants or manufacturers; Bellini's early career was to depend, after all, on an individual noble patron, as had the careers of his father and grandfather.

He had a musician's traditional start: father and grandfather were both members of the craft.

The grandfather, Vincenzo Tobia Bellini, came from a high hill town in the Abruzzi, far away on the mainland; after graduating from one of the celebrated Naples music schools, he moved to Catania as resident composer-organist to a great nobleman, Prince Biscari, married a Sicilian widow, and settled down to a middling career, locally circumscribed. Biscari, his chief employer, was a leader of Catanese intellectual life. His palace housed a noted museum of ancient art, as well as a (less important) theatre that sometimes gave opera; it was the meeting-place for Freemasons – the conscious agents of enlightenment. Vincenzo Tobia, it has been suggested, may have written music for Masonic functions, and may himself have been a Mason; but we lack evidence. His main task undoubtedly was to provide church music, not specially individual but adequate for the many functions that marked the religious year.

Vincenzo Tobia's career overshadowed that of his son and assistant Rosario Bellini, Vincenzo's father. The Catania corporation's award of a scholarship to the seventeen-year-old Vincenzo pointedly referred to his grandfather's 'merits' and his father's 'hard work'. Rosario was a mediocre artist; though he married a woman from a family of minor officials, Agata Ferlito, they seem to have lived as poor relations. Vincenzo, their first child, was born in a mezzanine flat of three small rooms under low arched ceilings, squeezed into a noble palace in central Catania. After three more sons and three daughters had been born they moved in 1813 to a cheaper flat; the rapid inflation of the Napoleonic wars may have impoverished them. For lack of space – and because of the musical promise he had shown – Vincenzo went to live with his grandfather. As an adult, permanently away from Catania, he was to correspond not with his parents but with his maternal uncle Vincenzo Ferlito.

These arrangements point to nothing like a rift in the family. Grandfather, father, and maternal uncle lived within a few streets of each other and, no doubt, in each other's pockets. In later years, the adult Vincenzo explicitly meant his letters to be shared among all at home. If he wrote to his uncle that was probably because his parents found letter-writing difficult: his mother's signature is that of a barely literate person (one of his sisters could not write at all), and Rosario's business letters after Bellini's death are awkwardly phrased. Young Vincenzo's living with his grandfather stemmed from his informal musical apprenticeship: after the seven-year-old boy had composed a *Tantum ergo* for church performance – so runs one of the unnamed chronicler's more believable tales – his grandfather said 'If you study I'll teach you three times a week.' There is no sign in Vincenzo's life of anything other than intense Mediterranean family feeling. We catch an echo of it in the buzz of Sicilian pet names: he was Vincenzuddu, Nzuddu, Nzudduzzu; in 1832, with the success of *Norma* behind him, he was still sending 'lots of kisses to

Papa, Mama, my sisters, brothers, boy cousins, girl cousins, in particular Pudda and Zudda, Zia [Aunt] Saruzza, Zia Mara, Zia D[onna]
Judda, etc. etc. etc.'

What did Bellini get from his family? Genetically, his celebrated
good looks: as an adult he was tall, with curly fair hair and blue eyes –
Sicilian traits, though of a minority. Musically his family gave him
early habituation and practice. Even if we discard the absurd stories,
he must have started playing the piano and composing by the age of
five or six. Music was everyday life.

What did he get from his native city? For him it was, in effect, Sicily: there is no record of his having left Catania till he went to Naples
at seventeen. To a young musician it offered plenty of church music
(solo or choral, often accompanied by organ or orchestra), intermittent opera – Catania still lay on the fringe of the Italian opera circuit –
military band music, and private music-making we know little
about. We know little more about the folk songs Vincenzo may have
heard; at one time these were thought to have influenced him, but
both in Catania and, later, in Naples folk and theatre music were so
entangled as to make influences hard to pin down. Barrel organs, for
instance – young Vincenzo is said to have loved the early bellows-
driven type – may well have played theatre tunes.

Folk musicians he undoubtedly heard were the peasants from the
far side of Etna who, every Advent, came into town with their bag-
pipes. According to the musicologist Salvatore Enrico Failla, Bellini
got three things from them. First, their improvised melodies helped
to shape those he was to become famous for – seemingly meandering
and unpredictable. Then the balance of distance and attraction
between drone and chanter was to influence his handling of accompaniment and melody. Finally, the music of these southern pipes
(more guttural than Scottish ones) encouraged in Bellini's accompanied melodies a tendency to slip into the modal, into chromaticisms,
and into oscillations between major and minor. The Mediterranean
plangency of Bellini's slow music, though distilled into 'high' culture, had its roots in the folk.

About Bellini's general education we know little. He worked at home with individual teachers, mostly priests. The unnamed relative already mentioned is here at his most blatant, alleging studies in Greek, English, and philosophy of which later life shows not a trace. Bellini's grown-up letters in their at times awkward, incorrect Italian witness to a skimpy literary education and few literary interests. He never mentions reading anything other than an opera libretto or material for one; rare mentions of Coriolanus and Socrates (as examples of prophets without honour) or of ancient Tyre (as a parallel to modern London) suggest a dusting of Plutarch occasionally shaken out.

This was nothing out of the way. Music even now is a demanding art; it tends to monopolize those who practise it. Artisan musicians like Bellini's father and grandfather and many others worked unquestioningly at their trade. Vincenzo was to grow more self-aware as an artist, but only in his last two years in Paris would he live alongside men like Berlioz and Liszt who brought into music the concerns of literature, politics, and philosophy; only after his death would an Italian musician – Verdi – engage seriously with Shakespeare and Hugo. In this as in much else Bellini was the last flower of the old Italian school.[4]

Artisan-like though his schooling largely was, Bellini acquired social graces that lifted him out of artisan status. Near the end of his life he explained to his uncle his 'system' of 'always approaching the very best society' wherever he lived – in Naples, Milan, London, Paris – and establishing himself among them. This meant getting on outwardly equal terms with aristocrats. He seems to have begun in Catania. His looks helped, but he must have worked at his manners and his clothes in ways we can only guess at.

Amid the little we know of his adolescent life one episode suggests a good deal. He was playing at a reception together with one of the sons of Prince Cassaro, a former government minister; when Bellini criticized the son's flute playing the young man joshed him as 'Bruttini' ('ugly' – instead of 'pretty' – 'little things'). They were clearly on easy terms. At this reception Bellini came to the notice of the young man's married sister, the Duchess of Sammartino. The Duke was from 1818 governor of Catania province. The following year he in effect told the city corporation to award Bellini a scholarship; there is no sign that they were reluctant, but the initiative came from the Duke. Bellini's 'system' had paid off.

This scholarship – of 36 ounces (about £24) a year for four years – took up some two-fifths of the money the corporation gave out each year to aspiring artists, for instance painters and sculptors. Bellini petitioned for it on the grounds that his family was poor and he needed to form his 'taste' and 'principles' in the music college at Naples, the capital of the new united kingdom of the Two Sicilies. The award stipulated that if he did not afterwards live in Catania he must return the money, but this condition was not in the event enforced. On 5 June 1819 Bellini set off overland for Messina to visit a paternal aunt and her family and then take ship for Naples.

For him that was the last of Sicily as anything but a place to visit. He was to make an ill-documented 'surprise' trip in 1824 or 1825, near the end of his studies, and a triumphal return in 1832. But he never worked there: it was too far out of the operatic mainstream. Donizetti did work in Palermo in 1825–6, but that was in his journeyman phase – a phase Bellini was to skip. In 1819, however, and for some time afterwards, Bellini seemed set to come back and repeat his grandfather's career as a well-regarded local musician: that was still the outcome assumed in 1822, when Catania corporation extended his scholarship to run until 1826. Only the success of his graduation opera was to make him a long-term emigrant, of the kind who had gone to make his fortune and would not for many years settle back home. It had always been understood that after his training he would help to maintain his family; and so he was to do, with remittances from Milan and Paris rather than with a cathedral salary.

Sicily then lived in his mind as the place of home and family. Years later he delighted in meeting a young Catanese acquaintance: 'I'm so happy I'm beside myself' (literally 'out of my shirt'); Catania, they agreed, was the finest place in the world, its patron Saint Agatha 'the first saint in heaven', and they ended by shouting in unison 'Viva Sant'Agata!'. But if Bellini took any interest in Sicilian events we know nothing of it. On occasion he called himself a Sicilian, but his boast that his first two professional operas were set in the island was at least in part flattery of a high official, and his passing self-identification with Sicilian pride or hot-headedness did little more than endorse clichés. His feeling was genuine; but it homed in on childhood and first youth.

With him on the journey to Naples Bellini took a sheaf of his early compositions, most of them deliberately written over the previous year to show the authorities at the music college what he could do. They seem not to have greatly impressed his new teachers, who put him in the beginners' class. Bellini may have suffered the disappointment of the frog from a small pond.

Whether he took with him memories of other than family feelings we do not know. A branch of the posthumous myth in Catania burgeoned with tales of Vincenzo's sexual exploits – one told years later by a friend (who also brought out 'remembered' verses and an obviously faked letter), others without visible source. Among the girls mentioned were a pupil of his father's and a lay sister in a convent, abetted by the nuns. All these stories sprang, as far as we can tell, from the imaginative needs of the Catania male public. In one alleged intrigue Vincenzo would have been twelve years old, while in another the girl would have been seven or eight.

The truth is that we know nothing of Bellini's erotic life before 1822, and very little before 1828. For many young bourgeois males in late nineteenth-century Italy, sexual initiation came in the late teens, from a servant or prostitute and without commitment; but this perhaps tells us little about Catania in the 1810s. It was after all a place where men and women were segregated in church. Soon after his arrival at Naples Bellini wrote a letter in which we glimpse an ingenuous boy.

It is addressed to his uncle at Messina, with whose family he had stayed; one of its members was his young cousin Cristina. He thanks God that the family are over their illnesses:

> Just one thing bothers me – that D[onna] Cristina has given up music. She has a piano, and it sleeps, while here I would have wished for one to raise my spirits. I was to have bought a clavichord, but I couldn't find one. They do make small pianos, but they want blood money for them. And here is my cousin who thinks nothing of that fine instrument of hers. God sends bread to those who have no appetite.

He then tells his aunt that he has not yet bought her the French muslin she asked for, because in the summer Neapolitan women wear white and the fashionable colours will not be known till the autumn (31 July 1819). The naive hope that his uncle might send him the unused piano comes through so clearly that we see the adolescent scowl. In the event, Bellini was to acquire a piano – shared with his friend Florimo – only five years later.

For a seventeen-year-old musician from Catania, studying at the Naples college was the highest mark he could aim at. The state, the city, and the college were as far as you could hope to go.

Rule from Naples had irked some Palermo nobles and intellectuals: under the old Spanish empire the kingdoms of Sicily and Naples had both been ruled from Madrid, but separately. For good or ill, however, Neapolitans and Sicilians dealt far more with each other than either did with people from the north; in the year of Bellini's death a person travelling from Naples to Florence could still be said to 'go to Italy'. The city of Naples, by far the biggest in the peninsula (and one of the biggest in Europe), had not yet become notorious as a sink of crime and disease; the poverty of many of its inhabitants struck tourists as picturesque, with at most a twinge if they called to mind the bloody part the mob had played in several revolts, lately (in 1799) at the expense of the high-minded republican leaders briefly installed by the French. Tourists came for the antiquities, the volcano, the bay, the climate, and the pursuit of pleasure, above all through music.

During the eighteenth century Naples had overtaken Venice as the headquarters of Italian music; this meant in the first place opera, with oratorio a strong second. Not that the kingdom as a whole had a first-class opera network. The hinterland was too poor: opera as a profession and a business was focused on northern Italy. The city of Naples, however, was where the court and the nobility of the whole kingdom lived; the concentrated resources drawn from taxes and rents enabled its theatres to give opera year in year out, with only brief pauses for religious festivals. As a matter of policy the Bourbon kings made the royal theatre, the San Carlo, the biggest in the world; true, its artists were many of them imported. What did most to feed Naples's reputation as musical capital were its four colleges (*conservatorii*, originally orphanages) – all religious foundations and nurseries of celebrated singers and composers.

When Bellini arrived in 1819 the San Carlo was at the height of its splendour thanks to a royal subsidy unmatched in the peninsula. This sprang from a gambling monopoly: the manager of the San Carlo, who ran the gambling, handed part of the takings to the crown and got a subsidy on top of his share of the profits. The monopoly had arisen under the previous Napoleonic government, whose lavish patronage had also brought in some French neoclassical opera by Gluck and Spontini; it was to be abolished after a revolution in 1820. Rossini, in the fifth year of his stay as resident composer – and partner in the gambling concession – was using these resources to launch a string of boldly planned serious operas.

Musical education, however, was still recovering from the severe economic crisis that had struck it in the late eighteenth century. The four colleges had run seriously into debt, perhaps because inflation had eaten into their fixed incomes from investments. They had in the end been reorganized into a single new college, no longer ecclesiastical or in part charitable but a government institution with students in semi-military uniform. This college was housed in the ex-convent of San Sebastiano, a building that has long since been pulled down. Here Bellini was to live and work for almost eight years.

This is the least known period of his life. We have only three unin-
formative letters besides the petition with which, in September 1819
– soon after his arrival – he asked for and got a free place at the Conservatorio: in effect an extra scholarship, this time from the government. At the same time he got out of the beginners' class.

We therefore depend almost wholly on Francesco Florimo, writing and editing in old age as custodian of two myths, that of Bellini
and that of the Neapolitan musical school. In dealing with the Conservatorio years Florimo is at his most problematic: there the two
myths came together, and he was unreliable on both. At the time,
however, he was fellow-student, eyewitness, and confidant.

About the Conservatorio we do know something. Reorganization
had not altered its basic character or its teaching methods. As a self-
perpetuating group of musicians it was deeply conservative and was
to remain so for many years.

Conservatism marked both its teaching and its musical outlook.
Because it was a college we tend to think of it as an institution with a
collective leadership and agreed curriculum, methods, and standards. In practice, every teacher ran his own 'school'. His relation to
his pupils was paternal: they would defer to him and kiss his hand as
he came in. He would help them or tell them off as he thought fit;
under him he had pupil teachers (maestrini) who passed on his direc-
tions. Bellini, a student above the formal maximum age for entry,
became a maestrino on getting his free place.

Teaching was mostly one-to-one; in vocational music teaching it
is almost bound to be, and the college was nothing if not vocational:
'literary' instruction, though part of the course, was subordinate.
Students practised their instruments or voices most of the time indi-
vidually but alongside many others in large barrack-like rooms; they
learned to shut their ears to the din. There were also collective
rehearsals, twice weekly for voices and instruments separately and
once a week for everyone. The one real novelty was that students no
longer performed in churches.

The eighteenth-century tradition of the college ruled its leading teachers – all former pupils. They might disagree about which Neapolitan composer was most to be revered – Cimarosa or Paisiello in the immediate past, Durante or Leo in earlier decades – but to all of them the Naples school embodied true musical values: when the artistic director, Niccolò Zingarelli, brought in the study of Haydn and Mozart alongside the hallowed Neapolitan masters this struck one of his older colleagues as deplorable 'licence'.

Bellini's main teachers were, first, the septuagenarian Giovanni Furno for harmony, then Giacomo Tritto – aged eighty-six when Bellini arrived – and finally the autocratic Zingarelli himself, another septuagenarian. These were all composers, in ascending order of importance as contemporaries saw them; all are now forgotten. Tritto, most of whose works had been comic operas, none the less insisted on the study of counterpoint. When Bellini shifted to Zingarelli's class it was, according to Florimo, because Tritto did not suit his melodic bent, according to Bellini himself, because Tritto had died (aged ninety-one); both may be true. Bellini in later life gave his allegiance to Zingarelli; a few weeks before his death he commented, 'It's true that poor old man has his faults' (presumably his well-known surliness), 'but he deserves all the respect and affection of his students' (18 July 1835). Zingarelli thought well of his pupil: he made him in 1824 *primo maestrino* – head prefect, with a room of his own – and later gave him the privilege of writing a graduation opera. Florimo's story that he once snapped at Bellini 'you were not born for music' (with Bellini reminding him of it years later, after the success of *Norma*) is highly suspect: Florimo – we have seen – liked to invent dramatically apt prophecies and reversals.

We do not know what dealings Bellini may have had with Girolamo Crescentini, the famous castrato and teacher of singing, who joined the Conservatorio in 1825, aged a mere sixty-three and on a salary equal to Zingarelli's – whence an undying feud. Crescentini shortly prophesied that Bellini's second student opera would be a flop, so the chances are that in this southern world of personal loyalties they were never close. Zingarelli and Crescentini, however, did agree on what made for good vocal and musical style. Both detested the brilliant reigning composer of the moment, Rossini, and wished to go back to the plainer style of a quarter-century earlier, when the reigning composer had been Paisiello and the reigning emotion pathos, gentle or dignified. Zingarelli pointed his student the same way.

This was not just a matter of personal taste. Carping at Rossini was a Neapolitan habit. Elsewhere in Italy, too, a persistent line of criticism brought several objections against him: he took little notice of words, overloaded the vocal line with ornaments, and drowned it in noisy 'German' orchestration. The ideal was to make the vocal line expressive of the words, with discreet, minimal accompaniment: this, according to the brainier critics (who harked back to the ancient Greeks), made for truly 'philosophical' music.

The trouble was that in these Naples years Rossini – with one or two setbacks – carried all before him. By the time he left the city in 1822 the craze for his operas was breaking out all over Europe. The fizz and speed of his music might be un-'philosophical', even a trifle vulgar, but it was what the post-revolutionary audience wanted.

Zingarelli was scornful. He could afford to be: he had written the last of his thirty-eight (mostly serious) operas in 1811 and was devoting himself to sacred music and to teaching. According to Florimo, he made Bellini invent daily vocal melodies, and stressed that a composition must 'sing' if it was to touch the heart and please the audience: elaborate harmony and counterpoint would never do that. Students must learn the 'grammar' of music and then do their utmost to conceal it.

So overwhelming, though, was Rossini's triumph that Zingarelli's own students could not help imitating him all through the 1820s – Bellini too, though he was the most resistant and the first to break away. The tension between the old-school ideal they had imbibed and the new practice that had run away with them still shows in Florimo's comments half a century later: he exalts Rossini as the great genius of Italian music, yet he writes that the school represented by

Bellini's student operas, though 'not the one about to predominate', was 'reformed on natural principles . . . plain, gentle, full of feeling, melancholy . . . [with] the great secret of pleasing spontaneously rather than through artifice'. 'Artifice' can only be a dig at Rossini.

Paisiello, held up as ideal, certainly influenced Bellini: the deliberate simplicity of Nina, Paisiello's smiling-through-tears opera of 1789 about a girl who goes mad for love, stands behind La sonnambula; Bellini cited it as a model for Elvira in I puritani. More dubious is Florimo's account of his friend's reverence for the older Jommelli and especially Pergolesi. The story of his copying out Haydn quartets and Mozart quintets has some corroboration in the printed music Bellini left behind in Naples, which included Mozart symphonies. (His alleged poring over a vocal septet by the young Donizetti, on the other hand, is part of Florimo's exceedingly suspect attempt to show a Bellini full of warm regard for his future rival.) Largely undocumented, but perhaps most important in shaping Bellini's musical taste, is his experience of opera in Naples theatres.

As primo maestrino from 1824 Bellini was entitled to go to the San Carlo twice a week (no doubt on a free pass), but as plain maestrino he could probably go to the theatre well before that: two of Florimo's anecdotes, for what they are worth, depend on his having attended the San Carlo in 1820 and the shabbier Nuovo in 1822.

At the San Carlo, the only theatre for which we have detailed programmes, Rossini's operas held sway. Semiramide, his culminating Italian opera, was given in all seasons between 1823 and Bellini's departure in 1827. Florimo remembered an awestruck Bellini pausing on the way back to college after the performance to ask whether it was any use going on with music; this is plausible, for Semiramide was a compendium of what Italian opera had achieved. From it (and from Mosè in Egitto and Maometto II, both done more than once during his stay) he could learn above all how to organize a mighty and complex ensemble, with soloists and chorus deployed to strike into the listener classic emotions of pity and terror. Here is one obvious source of Bellini's own culminating achievement, the final scene of Norma;

another – a local speciality – was Spontini's monumental Paris opera *La vestale*, its austere vocal line now declaimed by Joséphine Fodor, a fine singer who also appeared as Semiramide.

There were, besides, several operas by the older composers Johann Simon Mayr and Pietro Generali, and by young imitators of Rossini – Saverio Mercadante, Michele Carafa, Giovanni Pacini, and Gaetano Donizetti; the last also wrote comic and sentimental operas for other theatres. The Italianized Bavarian Mayr had helped to work out many of the structures of Italian opera that are attributed to Rossini. Bellini later wrote 'my heart owes its way of feeling to the study I made of [Mayr's] sublime compositions, full of true passion and tears': that was in a letter meant to be read out to the good-hearted, near-blind old composer who had befriended him, but it may have been only a slight exaggeration (25 August 1835). Mayr's *Medea in Corinto*, given at the San Carlo with Fodor, was another model for *Norma*, in its 'sublime' neo-classical declamation rather than in what may now seem weak melodies and quirkily elaborate orchestration. As for the coming young men, Pacini and Donizetti, they were Bellini's potential rivals: that, as we shall see, meant war.

For Bellini and his fellow-students opera was the field of choice. Their teachers, however, made them write sacred and, on a small scale, instrumental music; it was also easier to have sacred works performed. We therefore have from the young Bellini's hand – some written in Catania, some at Naples – four masses (Kyrie and Gloria only), over a dozen shorter religious works for solo voices and cho-rus, an organ sonata, nine songs or arias (one published in 1824 but written three years earlier), a wedding cantata, six two-part over-tures (slow-fast), and a tiny oboe concerto, the only survivor of a group of concertos written as exercises; fragments remain of con-certos for violin, flute, and bassoon, and some works are lost.

Would it make much difference to Bellini's standing if all this music were lost? He is the Italian composer most wholly identified with opera. None of this early work has so far impressed modern lis-teners as Rossini's string sonatas have (composed at the age of twelve); true, we seldom hear it performed. The oboe concerto is a charming trifle that could be by Cimarosa. The young Catanese was a precocious musician, 'talented but inexpert' in Andrew Porter's phrase; he took time to find his voice.

That voice began to be heard in his graduation opera, composed, as a good student was sometimes allowed to do, for the Conservatorio's small theatre, with all the parts sung by students – hence by male voices, some singing falsetto. *Adelson e Salvini*, a 'semi-serious' opera of peculiarly Neapolitan type, was first given in 1825, and was a success. As a result Bellini won the further privilege, open to the best students, of having an opera performed at the San Carlo.

Bianca e Fernando, a serious opera, was to have been given on 12 January 1826 at a gala for the heir to the throne, but because that date was the birthday of the late king court etiquette put it off till 30 May and necessitated a change of cast; to avoid a seeming allusion to the prince's name, 'Fernando' in the title was changed to 'Gernando' – a further bit of etiquette, much scoffed at by modern writers, though it was common form and went back at least to Metastasio's libretto *L'isola disabitata* of 1754. When *Bianca* in turn was a success Bellini had arrived. He went on living in the college (from autumn 1826 at its present site, the delightful rococo ex-convent of San Pietro a Majella) till he left for Milan and La Scala on 5 April 1827, but he was now a professional composer.

About his daily life in Naples we know remarkably little. The city was and is one of the liveliest, a collective theatre as well as a place of learning and thought, but what it meant to him is a blank. He secured the friendly patronage of the Duke and Duchess of Noja – the Duke was governor of the college and superintendent of theatres, an important person – but patronage it was and remained. He dedicated a song to another aristocratic lady. If his 'system' of pursuing noble connections scored any other hits we do not know of them. In the world of opera he came to know the Cottrau family, Franco-Neapolitan music publishers, and the leader-conductor of the fine San Carlo orchestra, Giuseppe Festa.

Anecdotes of college life are scarce and amount to little more than the odd feast on chops to eke out the institutional food. A moment of seeming political fervour came with the short-lived 1820 revolution. This was set off by the Carbonari, a secret society of democratic outlook, organized like the Masons in lodges. Bellini and Florimo joined one of the lodges. King Ferdinand I played for time, endured parliamentary government, but in the end connived at the Austrian army's restoring his own despotic rule. At that point the administrative director of the Conservatorio, a priest, called in Bellini and Florimo, told them their secret was known, and gave them a wigging: if they were not to go to gaol they must go first to confession, and then to the San Carlo and shout 'Long live our King Ferdinand, anointed by God and by right!' They did just that, but they would not inform on fellow-members. So runs Florimo's anecdote. It is plausible enough. What biographers have failed to point out is that at the height of the revolution about one adult male in five joined the Carbonari. The lodges had become a mixture of establishment and craze: Bellini's joining may not have meant much.

Throughout his life Bellini seems to have felt the need of a surrogate family. In Naples he and Florimo knew one called Andreana, with several sons and daughters of more or less their own age, intimately enough to be aware that one of the daughters was tubercular and missed some of her periods in consequence. A year after Bellini's departure relations went sour. The ultimate cause was what he regarded as the Andreanas' snobbery, worthy of 'half a century ago': Florimo, he wrote (May 1828), should 'make them understand that nowadays people esteem men of merit and who know how to love, rather than wealth and noble blood'. (The 'career open to talent', a theme launched by the French Revolution, was a good deal in the minds of young men on the make.) It sounds as if either he or Florimo had proposed to one of the daughters and been rebuffed, but the evidence is obscure.

Bellini famously did wish to marry a Neapolitan girl and was rebuffed. This was Maddalena Fumaroli, daughter of a judge. We have seen that once he left Naples he lost interest, though she for some time did not; and that news of her death brought a fit of real though not overwhelming grief.

For the Naples story we depend on Florimo. He made a meal of it. Some of his detail is false: of two Bellini songs, allegedly to words by Maddalena, the words of one at least were by somebody else, and both were composed before – on Florimo's own showing – the young people had met. The neat dramatic reversal may be false too (the judge, having several times turned away a penniless beginner, relents after Bellini's early triumphs at La Scala; Bellini says no but promises to marry no one else). Bellini's letters neither disprove nor support it.

The kernel of the story is as ordinary as can be, though that does not lessen the suffering of the young people, especially the young woman. Bellini meets Maddalena at her father's house, offers to teach her singing; they fall in love; her parents stop the lessons and ask Bellini gradually to stop his visits. The young people keep up a clandestine correspondence; after the success of each of his student operas Bellini hopefully proposes through an intermediary, but is each time refused. He then leaves Naples, after a secret interview at which both weep 'unrestrained and heart-rending' tears.

Something like this no doubt occurred. The judge was bound to refuse an offer from a young man just entering upon a highly insecure profession. The young man was almost bound to cool once he had moved to a city where letters from Naples took eight days to arrive, and where he was surrounded by exciting new people – if, that is, he had not cooled earlier.

Such was Bellini's romance. Seven years on, he could look back with feeling. It was, he reminded Florimo, the anniversary of the day when they had run after 'a certain carriage'; next day Judge Fumaroli had complained to the college authorities and they had got another wigging: 'isn't that right?' They had stood on the waterfront 'by divine moonlight: isn't that right? Oh sweet thoughts and innocent age of illusion, how you've vanished!!! And yet I am not now unhappy.'

With Mediterranean realism he went on to tell Florimo briefly of his current, unromantic, undemanding liaison (4 August 1834).

Soon after his departure from Naples Maddalena's love had become a bore. In the first half of 1828 he put off answering her insistent letters, wished she would come round; he hoped all would end well for her – 'for my part I could never have made her happy, because that's what the needs of my career and my finances dictate' (16 January 1828). Almost certainly true; but it is embarrassing to have to explain loss of love.

No such embarrassment marked the central relationship of Bellini's life, that with Florimo. Theirs were, Bellini wrote, 'hearts made only to be friends to the last breath' (12 January 1828); 'your existence is necessary to mine' (23 January 1828); 'my excellent, my honest, my angelic friend! . . . The more we know of the world the more we shall see how rare is our friendship' (11 February 1835): a brief sample.

Such evidence, Herbert Weinstock wrote in 1971, 'inescapably suggest[s] to modern readers a homosexual attachment'. He should have said 'to modern readers who know nothing of Mediterranean societies and little of the world of early nineteenth-century Italian opera'. Post-Freudian knowingness obfuscates; closer knowledge helps.

Francesco Florimo (1800–88), a year older than Bellini, came from a small town in the southernmost tip of Calabria, an area historically bound up with Messina more than with the Kingdom of Naples. That did not keep him from ranting on occasion against everything Sicilian, or Bellini from joshing him as *stupidino, Calabresino*. Indeed their quarrels were long remembered by fellow college students, and flared up from time to time in their correspondence. When both were in Palermo in 1832 Florimo met Bellini's Sicilian friends, who then mocked at him and made him out to be disloyal; Bellini, in a dignified letter, reproved them: 'others may be found to equal [him], but none to surpass him in affection for his true friends' (24 September 1832).

Both were young southern provincials on the make, in a capital still dominated by the aristocracy and by royal officials and lawyers. After graduation Florimo stayed on at the Conservatorio for the rest of his life, minding the library, acting as Bellini's alter ego, but never, though pressed to come, venturing to Paris or even Milan in his friend's lifetime. The two met again only when Bellini came south in the spring of 1832. After Bellini's death Florimo was treated as his spiritual heir.

Their friendship was indeed of a type hard for modern English-speaking readers to understand: demonstrative, fervent, lifelong, and normal. People familiar with pre-industrial Mediterranean or Indian society will know what to make of it. To call it homoerotic is literally true but unenlightening. To call it homosexual is to introduce a category people in the early nineteenth century did not bring to bear on such a relationship – even in England: compare Tennyson and Arthur Hallam. It therefore distorts. Physical homosexual relations were known (by most, abhorred); but people did not connect them with deep friendship.

Friendship was anyhow an inflated currency. In the world of opera a 'friend' could be someone you had not even met: it meant someone who did you a favour. The correspondence of singers, musicians, librettists, impresarios, and agents is full of protestations of friendship in this sense, or reproaches addressed to 'friends' who did not do the expected thing. Among those who really were on friendly terms 'Love me as I love you' was a common salutation. Deep friendship needed a still more fervent vocabulary.

What went on in Bellini's or Florimo's unconscious is beyond us – and was beyond them: so far beyond that Bellini could write what on the surface looks like a proto-Freudian analysis of his friend's feeling, but was in truth a naive observation.

When Bellini started his great affair with Giuditta Turina he told Florimo about it in detail. Florimo's reply was a joke: Bellini had no doubt lost weight. This hurt Bellini deeply:

I thought the heart of my dearest and only friend would be ready to receive the confidences of my heart; but after your insulting reply I shall know how to behave, and will give up all hope of being able to consider you my friend in the full sense of the term. True, I don't doubt that you love me wholeheartedly, but your behaviour, groundless, and directed merely by caprice, is too cruel and unfriendly. Enough: think as you wish, I have done a friend's duty . . . [added at the end:] I will never, never change (17 October 1828).

Florimo hastened to deny that he was hostile to the relationship with Giuditta. Bellini was pacified:

I'm very happy that you see nothing wrong with my relationship, though you have always been (and, unable as you are to change your nature, I think you still are) dead against any passionate love of mine, and I'm telling you this because it's plain and obvious in your [letter], where at one point you think the more highly of my lady friend because she is jealous of your friendship, and as indeed, believing your friendship for me to have about it something extraordinary, that too pleases me exceedingly (1 December 1828).

Bellini's syntax failed him, but his meaning is made clear by another letter (4 March 1829). Florimo had been so offensive as to doubt Bellini's affection for him; the best proof of the contrary was 'the jealousy you [Florimo] roused in G[iuditta], for, as you may well imagine, that could stem only from the incredible solicitude I showed for you'. Friend and mistress, in other words – as their mutual jealousy showed – both loved him and he loved both; all was well. By the time of the letter last quoted, Giuditta had 'become con- vinced that our friendship is brotherly and unbreakable, and she has almost got used to loving you as I do'. To Florimo's doubts Bellini replied: 'Do you understand or not? That in me love for you has become an element necessary to my peace, to my life? And that I don't want to hear about doubts, even though they are only an impulse of your love? Enough.'

We too had better leave it at that.

2 Storming La Scala

'I'll take you on.' So says the ambitious young provincial Eugène de Rastignac, Balzac's hero, as he looks down on Paris from the heights of Montmartre. Milan has no heights; but the young Sicilian composer could have felt much the same as he looked for the first time at the bland façade of La Scala. After his two prentice operas Bellini was going straight to the top, determined to succeed; and he did.

He had no contract, but in Naples he had been promised one by Domenico Barbaja, the reigning impresario there, who also had the management of La Scala in partnership with the Villa brothers. These men, and another impresario Bellini was to deal with later, Giuseppe Crivelli, had helped to turn Milan into the capital of Italian opera. Their device, one seldom connected with music, was the roulette wheel.

In the last years of the eighteenth century Naples was still the Italian city with the greatest musical prestige; Bologna was the headquarters of the opera profession, where many singers trained, agents congregated, and bargains were struck. Milan was an important date on the Italian opera circuit, but no more. With its surrounding region of Lombardy its administration and economy had benefited from the rule of 'enlightened' Habsburg sovereigns in Vienna – Maria Theresa and her sons. For operatic purposes, however, it mattered that those sovereigns were far away: the resident court was that of a mere viceroy. It mattered still more that they were reluctant to subsidize the pleasures of the rich or to encourage immoral behaviour. The gambling monopoly we have seen making for splendid opera seasons at Naples was abolished in Milan in 1788.

The French wars, however, brought many changes. From 1801 to 1814 Milan was the capital of a state ruled by Napoleon and called 'Italy' (it covered only the north-east of the peninsula). Almost continuous war, waged in central Europe rather than near by, meant that the city was full of troops with money to spend, and for some years enjoyed a new prosperity; the needs of war and taxation built up a middle class of educated officials. A hard-pressed government restored the gambling monopoly and handed it to the management of La Scala; it now included the roulette wheel, an innovation brought in from revolutionary France.

Barbaja – a near illiterate café waiter and billiard player – was the original roulette concessionaire; he, Crivelli, the Villas, and others in shifting partnerships, won the management of La Scala and ran it throughout the wars, down to 1814; after a period of crisis (the restored Austrian government abolished the gambling monopoly once more) they came back to it at various times from 1823 on. They were shady characters: Barbaja used the monopoly, while he had it, to take a cut from unlicensed private gambling; Crivelli hired thugs to beat up a man who forced him to pay a debt. Yet Barbaja at least, for all his illiteracy and bluster, was a man of taste who produced opera and ballet on a grand scale; the roulette money underwrote lavish stagings amid magnificent scenery. This, together with the prosperity of Milan, its middle-class audience, and its emergence after the wars as the chief centre of Italian intellectual life, established La Scala as the premier Italian opera house.

The theatre and the warren of streets around it now displaced Bologna and Naples as the heart of both Italian music and the opera profession. Just how close-knit the area was can only be imagined: much of it disappeared half a century later in the building of the Galleria. Singers, impresarios, music publishers lived there; Bellini too found lodgings within sight of the theatre.

Opera, galvanized by the success of Rossini, carried all before it.

4 La Scala and, in the background, the Contrada Santa Margherita where Bellini
first lodged in Milan. Contemporary print.

Church music was in decline. Audiences showed little interest in
instrumental music and knew little of the Vienna school; at most, the
leader of the La Scala orchestra played string quartets with a few
friends, and there were occasional performances of Haydn's *Creation*
and Beethoven's simpler works.

Opera seasons stood at the heart of social life for the aristocracy
and the new middle class: that was where they ate, drank, gossiped,
and met their friends. The chief seasons were carnival (in the traditional sense of the period of winter festivities running from 26
December until the onset of Lent), spring, and autumn. In each of
these seasons a theatre as prestigious as La Scala was expected to put
on at least one new opera, more often two; members of the audience
looked forward to each new work and, if they approved, might attend
it twenty times or more. These new works were turned out on a rapid,
demanding schedule by artists most of whom spent the rest of the
year going round the Italian opera circuit. That circuit now took in all

the chief towns of north and central Italy, Naples, the Sicilian cities, and leading theatres abroad – in Vienna, Paris, London, and the Iberian peninsula.

The timetable for rehearsal and composition was closer to that of Hollywood studios in the 1930s than to anything known in opera houses today. A novice composer would usually start, as Donizetti did, by writing operas for second-rank theatres. In early December he would simultaneously finish and rehearse the opera due to open the carnival season on 26 December, plan another for the spring season in another town, and discuss a third for the autumn yet elsewhere; he might work in a fourth at one of the summer seasons put on for trade fairs. A normal output was three or four operas a year. Bellini not only skipped this stage, he composed on average one opera a year.

How did he get to La Scala in one jump? After some initial trouble about his contract – the official supervisory board may have fussed about taking on a novice – Barbaja's local partners matched him with the best librettist available, Felice Romani, and the two got to work on an opera for the autumn 1827 season: in the event, *Il pirata*. Barbaja had plainly decided to take a chance on the fledgling composer after his student operas – if not after *Adelson e Salvini* in 1825, then after *Bianca e Fernando* in 1826.

There was good cause. *Adelson*, staged for the first time professionally in 1985, is accomplished in ways seldom thought Bellinian, yet marked here and there by his individual voice. Its original orchestration, pointed, graceful, and varied, shows a young composer who has studied good examples and does not rely on noise for effect. It confounds the late nineteenth-century view of Bellini as a naive melodist who did not know how to handle the orchestra. The layout shows good stage sense, though the big climax – the fire scene at the end of Act 2 – goes on too long. The vocal music is much of it efficient rather than characterful, but the tenor's final romanza with chorus and especially the soprano's opening aria ('Dopo l'oscuro nembo', later adapted as Juliet's opening aria in *Capuleti*) have the Bellinian fingermarks – 'long, long, long', plangent, undulating melodies that seem to feed on and renew themselves; the last section of the Adelson-Bonifacio duet has real drive in its anapaestic rhythm and inventive twists. Rossini's influence shows in the odd melisma and crescendo, but the presiding deity is Paisiello.

The trouble with *Adelson* is not so much the libretto as the genre. The original French story dated from the 1770s vogue for 'storm and stress', an early form of romanticism: in a fantasy Ireland where a vengeful robber lurks, two close friends fall out over a woman, one of them kills her, all come to a bad end. To force this into a Neapolitan 'semi-serious' libretto the hack Andrea Leone Tottola – working for an earlier composer – basted it with dialect comedy and stuck on an absurd happy ending. Shifts of tone jar; the genre was out of date in 1825 and has never recovered. Bellini revised *Adelson*, perhaps in 1826, for a commercial theatre, but turning the spoken dialogue into recitative and Italianizing the Neapolitan comedy merely dragged things out; it was not performed. He then recycled some pieces in his next four operas.[5]

Bianca e Fernando too suffers from perpetuating an outdated vogue, this time for 'rescue opera'. The theme of a noble character saved from imprisonment, perhaps from death, at a tyrant's hands was launched by the French Revolution; of the many works it inspired only Beethoven's *Fidelio* holds the stage. There, a wife's heroic love rouses basic emotions, but in *Bianca*'s libretto by a young Neapolitan amateur, Domenico Gilardoni (taken from a stage play), Eros is nowhere: all it offers is a father rescued by his son and daughter.

Bellini was now writing for the leading singers of the day. Henriette Méric-Lalande and G. B. Rubini sang the postponed Naples version; in spring 1828, after Bellini's triumph with *Pirata*, Adelaide Tosi and Giovanni David – originally scheduled to sing the leads in Naples – opened the new Teatro Carlo Felice in Genoa with a version a good deal revised yet not substantially altered in character or quality. Both versions met with fair success, in Genoa after some initial doubt, but neither got far on the opera circuit; once again Bellini reused material from them in his later works.

In *Bianca* the young composer had to work the new structures devised by Mayr and others and codified by Rossini. Here the basic unit is the double aria. It begins as a rule with an accompanied recitative to establish a mood, and goes on to a cantabile (emotion dwelt on and suspended); after a brisk middle passage – someone, perhaps the chorus, intervenes, brings news, or otherwise changes the situation – it discharges pent-up feeling in a (usually) faster cabaletta, with a chance in the second verse for brilliantly ornamented display, and, often, a hammering coda shaped to elicit applause. The same pattern in more complex form – fast-slow-fast, meditation-resolution – informs duets and other ensembles as well as the climax of the big finale that generally closes the first half.

Bellini showed that he could handle the new routine, but routine is where much of *Bianca* stays. The overture, with anguished string figuration over a relentless bass, has real thrust; other passages that need to work up excitement, such as the recognition trio, are plain inadequate. Rossini's influence brings crescendos and ornamental vocal cascades at Bianca's entrance aria; to better effect, occasional attempts at shaping the new structures into continuous music drama. The Bellinian fingermarks again show; the 'strongest link' really is strong – and it dates from the original version. This is the soprano heroine's G minor romanza 'Sorgi, o padre' (with poignant clarinet and harp accompaniment and brief interventions by the contralto). The intense, sinuous, faintly folk-like melody opens out at the end, by again and again eluding the cadence at the last moment, onto an upland C major, time suspended until the minor returns to deepened pathos. Here was a new voice.[6]

With these two works behind him, the young composer needed favourable conditions to make a decisive mark at La Scala. That meant good singers and a good libretto; in 1827 it also meant a vehicle for the high romantic emotions Italian audiences had begun to favour.

We have almost no evidence for the months between Bellini's arrival in April 1827 and the first night of *Il pirata* on 27 October. He perhaps did not need to insist on good singers – the soprano and tenor from the Naples Bianca, Méric-Lalande and Rubini, were under contract at La Scala together with the supremely elegant bass-baritone Antonio Tamburini – but if he behaved then as he did later, he must have had a hand in the choice both of Felice Romani as librettist and of a romantic subject.

Romani and Bellini were to collaborate on all but one of Bellini's operas. Theirs, it has often been said, was an ideal partnership. This too, however, is in part myth. Its propagators were the self-important Romani himself in his obituary of Bellini; much later, Romani's widow and Florimo. The widow's motives were plain and the swollen share she allotted her husband has generally been discounted. Florimo, however, was believed; we have seen how he invented new matter that made Bellini appear to fawn on his librettist when he had done no such thing. Florimo's motive is obscure; perhaps his inventions satisfied his dramatic sense.

The matter is not clear-cut. On the one hand we know from authentic letters that Bellini set a high value on Romani and was keen to work with him. Even when he had much cause to complain of Romani's behaviour he pointed out in a letter to a disinterested third party the librettist's chief merit – 'Romani's fine diction, clear, and yet not common . . . it vibrates and touches the heart' (1 July 1835). Early on, when Bellini put forward possible subjects for an opera and Romani chose *La straniera* as the likeliest, that settled the matter: 'there's no going back on a Romani' (24 September 1828). On the other hand we have to discard as suspect expressions attributed to Bellini (and quoted by every biographer) in 'letters' to Florimo for which no autograph has ever been seen.[7]

What Bellini did with the words of an opera libretto is central to his achievement; his way with Italian is as distinctive as Purcell's with English, and may explain why, like Purcell, he is seldom fully understood by those who do not speak his language.

From *Il pirata* on, some Italian writers praised his music as 'philosophical' because – unlike Rossini's – it was unfailingly expressive of the words and did not subordinate them to a formal musical scheme. Bellini never committed himself to their theories, though he may have taken their arguments on board. Indeed he never commented on an opera as an integral work of art; when he dealt with his own works he treated them as a string of arias, duets, and other numbers, each with its merits, problems, and effect. The one time he stated what a libretto should be like was the one time he had to work with someone other than Romani – a poet with no theatrical experience, who held fast to the so-called rules of good verse. Opera, Bellini told him, must banish both musical and literary artifice:

> Carve in your head in adamantine letters: *Opera must make people weep, feel horrified, die through singing.* It's wrong to want to write all the numbers in the same way, but they must all be somehow shaped so as to make the music intelligible through their clarity of expression, at once concise and *frappante* [striking] (May 1834).

In another famous passage Bellini allegedly set out his method: he started from the words and declaimed them to himself till a melody formed in his mind. This 'letter', produced by a Sicilian friend, is an obvious and generally acknowledged fake. Several modern writers have none the less upheld its substance on the grounds that the friend must have got it from Bellini in conversation: this in the face of Bellini's well-documented habit of composing melodies – what he called 'motives', 'ideas', or 'daily exercises' as well as whole cabalettas – not just without a text but without even a subject for an opera, and of having words fitted to them later, not to mention his readiness to switch a melody from one text to another, very different one. He did work away at his themes and adapt them as he got the words: 'I've composed some beautiful phrases, which will be heightened according to the number they will go into' (12 May 1828); 'I hope, when I have the libretto, to place and develop them to good effect' (7 July 1828). But he was also prepared to torture pre-existing words with arbitrary repetition (as in Juliet's opening aria) to make them fit a pre-existing tune.

The notion of Bellini as a bard driven by verbal afflatus is absurd.

Even in the authentic letter of May 1834 just quoted, the role of clear
and striking words was to make the music 'intelligible'. Bellini seems
to have meant what Verdi was later to describe as *parola scenica*,
'stageworthy words' that would crystallize feeling in a musical
phrase. Music came first. The difference between him and Verdi was
that the later composer, with a far better literary education, could
suggest and even impose particular words on his librettist. Bellini
knew the words he needed when he saw them, but, it seems, could
not think them up himself.

For such a composer Romani's great merit was indeed his diction.
His words flow easily, they 'sing'; spare, little burdened with adjec-
tives, they tell. More dubious was his command of a drama as a
whole. In a twenty-one-year career as full-time librettist he wrote
some ninety librettos and dealt with some forty composers. The
quality of this output, not surprisingly, varied; he was also notorious
for being late. Romani, however, took a high line. He looked back to
Metastasio, the eighteenth-century poet whose librettos had enjoyed
greater prestige than the many composers who set them; he tried in
vain to publish his collected works as Metastasio had; he was apt to
preface a libretto with apologies to the effect that the 'unavoidable
circumstances' of the theatre had spoiled it; opera, he complained,
was now 'an overgrown child . . . the composer stretches it on a Pro-
crustes' bed . . . the singers turn it round and round at their whim . . .
and the audience tears it limb from limb like Orpheus at the hands of
the Bacchantes'. These allusions mirrored Romani's classicist habit
of mind: though he wrote librettos based on the tempestuous
romantic works of the new French school, he did his best to uphold
the classical ideal of poise and restraint.

Opera, however, had changed radically since Metastasio. Romani
might think of himself as a poet, his name might still figure on theatre posters ahead of the composer's, but in practice he had to work
like a hack. The cause was the Rossinian transformation. It brought
a new, shorter form of libretto, with fewer recitatives and more
ensembles (in which the words would be lost). It brought a faster

rhythm of production as well as a cult of novelty and surprise: a libretto must as a rule be written within forty days, and could be set only once or twice. Casts with fewer principals (three or four against the Metastasian five or six) might suddenly vary and require wholesale changes. Romani acknowledged this by demanding to know the cast before he would choose a subject or write; even then he sometimes had to write new words to fit pre-existing music, an act incongruous with his stance as a Metastasian poet. But while the vogue for opera raised singers' and composers' fees it did not bring higher payment for librettists. Romani was paid on average just under 750 francs for a libretto, and never more than 1,000 (compare Rossini's 5,000 francs for *Semiramide* in 1823, a figure Bellini would more than double by 1831). Theoreticians might go on about the primacy of words; the opera market had delivered its verdict.

The strain told on Romani. A craftsman who rewrote even when he was not made to, he took on too much of this ill-paid work; when he had four or five librettos on the stocks at once the result was several composers in despair, among them, on several occasions, Donizetti and Bellini. By his and Romani's second collaboration (on the revised portions of *Bianca e Fernando*) Bellini was feeling the anxiety he was to express again and again – 'if he doesn't give me words, I shan't be able to write music'. It did not help that Romani was full of specious explanations: the lateness, he would indignantly assert, was someone else's fault.

Romani gave composers a bad time. That they went back to him shows how much they thought of his work. Bellini too: when Romani was ill he was 'in an agony of fear that they might assign me another poet' (27 September 1828). Yet he liked to say that Romani worked better for him than for other composers because *he* gave his librettist a bad time. A libretto for Pacini was 'insipid'; a later one for Donizetti, *Lucrezia Borgia*, was clearly 'written for a composer who is not a *troublemaker* as Bellini was, who made poor Romani *write* and *rewrite* and so drove him to despair!!!' (23 January 1834). This need not be self-serving. *Lucrezia* is a poor libretto, and Bellini did for a time achieve a unique ascendancy over Romani, an established artist thirteen years his senior.

Romani dealt with Bellini – Alessandro Roccatagliati has shown – as with no other composer save Meyerbeer, a rich man and the exception to every rule. Their dealings were special in three ways. First, Bellini played a large part in determining the structure of an opera. Second, he and Romani worked together on the content and versification of individual numbers, like the three successive versions of the cabaletta to 'Casta diva' in *Norma*, each in a different metre; Bellini's hand wrote out parts of some drafts, which tells us not that he thought them up but that he and Romani were sharing a desk. Last, Romani almost from the start agreed to write words to fit Bellini's pre-existing melodies, a job he likened – after the two had fallen out – to torture.

Who chose the subject of *Il pirata* for Bellini's La Scala debut is not known. Romani's normal practice was to adapt a recent French work; the choice was sometimes his, sometimes the composer's. This time it fell on a French adaptation of Charles Maturin's *Bertram*, an English drama part gothic part romantic. Though Romani pared it down and Bellini threw out the wilder versions of the ending (either the hero jumped off a bridge or it collapsed under him), what was left was romantic in that it steeped the characters in extreme passions. As Friedrich Lippmann has observed, 'from the mouth [of Gualtiero, the pirate] we hear not one word that expresses a rational proposition'.

The story was romantic in other ways: it called up a faraway time and place (a Sicilian castle by the stormy Mediterranean during the thirteenth-century wars); it presented a doomed hero akin to Byron's outlaws, a nobleman turned pirate who finds his sweetheart has married his enemy; it sends him to execution, her into madness. As usual in Italian opera, however, history and local colour vanished into a prefatory note the audience might or might not read. This left a vague medieval atmosphere to be conjured up by the looming sets. The dramatic high spot was the scene in which Gualtiero threatens to kill Imogene's child; so successful was it that Romani and Bellini

– like Hollywood figures pleased with the latest twist in the Western – repeated it a few months later in the altered *Bianca e Fernando*.

If Bellini helped to choose the subject it would fit what we know of his behaviour in later years. The libretto, he then wrote, was 'the foundation of an opera'; choosing the story had become more difficult than writing the music; the need was for subjects that offered 'novelty' and 'interest' (14 February, [April] 1834). In his day 'novelty' and 'interest' meant romantic subjects. When, in 1829, Bellini was to write an opera for the new Parma theatre he shocked a pompous and classically minded official who fancied himself as librettist:

> this maestro's taste [the outraged official reported] runs to the romantic and the excessive. He told me the classical genre was cold and tedious. He took me to Vallardi's print shop to show me some lithographs he thought admirable, one in particular in which a father has his sons killed under his own eyes, pointing it out as a model of the most sublime theatrical effect. Unnatural encounters amid forests and tombs, and other such things, are the situations he delights in.

Bellini may have been pulling the man's leg, but he did share the contemporary taste for 'such things'. Even Romani told the Parma impresario that modern music called for 'strong situations, with a touch of the fantastic'. In practice his and Bellini's first two collaborations went furthest towards 'the romantic and the excessive', perhaps because it was, in Italy, the latest thing; the two men later chose to contain 'strong situations' in a renewed classical form. Bellini's death left blood and thunder to late Donizetti and Verdi.

Il pirata is the first of Bellini's operas to speak almost throughout in his individual voice. Rossini's scarcely appears; a critic praised the work for going back to 'beautiful simplicity', but it broke new ground as well.

Here Bellini first achieved a declamatory vocal line, little adorned, strongly expressive of the words, and backed by evocative use of the orchestra. Recitative moves into arioso, at times, as in Imogene's mad scene, highly dramatic. No wonder he was the Italian composer

5 Scene from *Il pirata*: Gualtiero threatens to kill Imogene's son. Contemporary print.

Wagner prized. A passage just before the Act 1 duet ('Perché cotanto io prendo') is startlingly Wagnerian. Imogene, who has not yet recognized the shipwrecked captain as her former lover, wonders why she feels such pity. Sequential orchestral phrases intersperse her declamatory line; they convey the agitation and sorrow she does not yet admit to herself. This likeness to Wagner's psychological use of the orchestra comes not by chance: Wagner, who in his youth conducted two Bellini operas and heard others, undoubtedly learned from him. Bellini's making the voice in such passages the lone actor is akin to the method of Greek tragedy as Italian critics imagined it: they thought the tragic actor had sung throughout to give the words maximum expression; Bellini's orchestra replaced the Greek chorus as commentator. In Wagner's *Ring* the notion of tragedy reborn comes to bloom.

Most of *Pirata* is not of course Wagnerian. Its finest stretches work into the Italian forms of the day a rare blend of energy and pathos. These are the opening arias for Gualtiero and Imogene, their duet, passionate, grand, and finely articulated, the Act 2 trio, and the mad scene at the end – the very numbers most applauded on the first night. Thanks to Rubini, Gualtiero's part has a high tessitura that speaks his continual excitement; it made Rubini, but is now hard to cast. Both it and Imogene's have fiery coloratura, dramatically apt to their overwrought state. The orchestral writing is varied: in the duet it goes from spare 'palpitating' comment to rapid driving rhythm to ostinato at the tense, forward-propelled 'Pietosa al padre', orchestra and voices then broadening out, anxiety set against unavowed love. The last scene deploys a masterful, spare array of instrumental means: a horn introduction, the long cor anglais lament with harp (could it have inspired the shepherd's lament in Act 3 of *Tristan und Isolde*?), a jagged, uncannily simple four-note string figure, and an oboe carrying the aria line, mark Imogene's desolation.

Among Bellinian fingermarks are the sense of emotional flux between the stanzas of Gualtiero's first aria, a series of modulations from G minor through several keys, minor and major; the noble line of Imogene's recitative-ariosos; the contrapuntal andante in the Act 1 finale, which combines different emotions yet saturates the whole in music; the floating melody that launches the trio; and, in the mad scene, both the 'inextinguishable' cor anglais tune and the seraphic cantabile of the aria. The finest music treats of love remembered in sorrow (at times in dreams), an essential Bellinian emotion.

If *Pirata* were all on that level it would be better known. Much of the baritone tyrant's part is four-square (though a good singer might make something of the duet), Gualtiero's Act 2 aria lacks character, the march and some fast passages are trivial, some accompaniments blatantly double the voices, and the chorus, with a large part, twice goes in for 'interesting' echo and pause effects that were deemed clever at the time but now suggest a young show-off out of his depth. All the same, the emotions are strong and clear and the work has a sweep that might well restore it to the opera house if one could find adequate singers – a big 'if'.

Il pirata was an immediate smash hit. Bellini, playing continuo (still the practice on the first three nights), was overcome at the applause and burst into convulsive sobs. 'Rejoice, yes, rejoice', he wrote to his family (29 October 1827). Joy did not stand in the way of level-headed appraisal. His situation was transformed; he decided then and there to stay on in Milan. If he had gone back to Naples he would have depended on one theatre and one overbearing manager; the north offered more chances of getting on.

His triumph with *Pirata* opened the doors of society, first in Milan and then in Genoa when the revised *Bianca e Fernando* inaugurated the new opera house on 7 April 1828; Bellini got to know Littas and Viscontis in Milan, Pallavicinos and Dorias in Genoa – highest aristocracy. In Genoa he also made friends with Napoleon's niece, wife of the British politician Lord Dudley Stuart. This acquaintance, chiefly with ladies, was perhaps superficial. Patronage still came into it: the young composer dedicated the vocal score of each opera to a duchess or countess and got a valuable watch as thanks. A more genuine upper-class friend – Bellini did not meet him until 1829 – was Alessandro Lamperi, a young official in the Piedmontese government at Turin; the friendship rested on a shared passion for music.

Far more important to Bellini was the surrogate family his teacher Zingarelli introduced him to in Milan. Francesco and Marianna Pollini were musicians in their sixties, childless, he a piano teacher, ex-singer, and minor composer, she a singer and harpist. Bellini was soon in and out of their flat every day, often stayed for meals, took their advice on matters great and small, and, later, was nursed by them through a serious illness; he became their 'dearest son'. Their few known letters, taken up mostly with theatre news, give little sense of their personality. They seem to have been affectionate, helpful people – what Bellini needed.

Another couple he made friends with, much nearer his age, were the great Milanese singer Giuditta Pasta and her husband Giuseppe, an amiable lawyer who had dropped a singing career to manage his wife's; according to one of the less suspect items in a letter published by Florimo, Bellini was on good terms with them by August 1828.

Giuditta Pasta

Cantante di Camera di S. M. I. R. A.

6 Giuditta Pasta in a heroic role. Somewhat flattering contemporary print.

7 Giuditta Turina. Pastel by Luigi Bianchi.

Pasta, then at the height of her fame as an incomparable singing actress, kept a base in Milan and a villa on Lake Como though she sang mainly in London and Paris. She had both a respectable family life (not always true of a prima donna) and many friends and interests outside the theatre (seldom true of a prima donna). Some of these friends were Italian liberals and their intellectual sympathizers abroad, like the novelist Stendhal. Her personality seems to have been calm and unremarkable, but for her and Giuseppe's habit of gender reversal in the nicknames and the very pronouns they used to each other; the sexual connotations may have been unconscious. Her great love was her daughter Clelia, aged ten in 1828, whom she was determined to shield from the world of the theatre: something that would matter to Bellini when, a few years on and after Giuditta had become his finest interpreter, he thought of marrying Clelia.

One of the people Pasta knew was another Giuditta, a young woman aged twenty-five in 1828 who came of one family of rich Lombard bourgeois, the Cantùs, and had married into another, the Turinas. In the slowly industrializing Lombardy of the time such families combined landowning and the professions with economic enterprise: Giuditta's husband Ferdinando Turina owned a silk mill on the family estate at Casalbuttano, in the plains of lower Lombardy; both the Turinas and the Cantùs had villas near Pasta's on Lake Como. Bellini met Giuditta Turina in April 1828 through a noble acquaintance in Genoa; by September she was his mistress – the only one known to us by name. The relationship was to last until 1833, and was not fully broken off for another year.

This, which one might think the central relationship in Bellini's life, is oddly elusive. The reason is in part that Florimo destroyed so many letters (and Turina must have destroyed others). But even when Turina and Bellini try to explain themselves in their surviving letters they perplex more than they enlighten. The explanations come after the breach: as often happens, particularly when estranged lovers are unused to searching their own motives, they seem to bring up pretexts unawares; the story does not ring true.

Florimo, however, chose not just to keep but to publish, eleven years after Turina's death, two letters in which Bellini told him about the start of the affair. He may have wished to present it at its freshest and draw a veil over the rest.

When the two were beginning to fall in love but had not yet embarked on the affair Bellini wrote that in Milan many women's names had been wrongly linked with his: all that had actually happened was 'a few *escapades*; but slight, short-lived things, and, I might say, already forgotten, because they did not engage my heart'. He was unsure what would come of his growing love, but in any case it might 'save me from a passion for an unmarried girl, which could land me with an eternal tie' (30 June 1828).

Both the slightness of the 'escapades' and the dread of rushing into an unsuitable marriage are characteristic; they come up in other letters to Florimo. The former we may readily believe. Unwelcome though the news would have been in Catania, Bellini was perhaps not highly sexed. To his uncle and to Florimo he wrote that he disliked 'low life'; he had always avoided dissolute people, gaming houses, and brothels. We need not doubt this. He was fastidious, in life as in dress. Nor is there any point (at least until his final Paris years) in asking who were the women concerned. The rumours bandied about at the time, mainly about singers, are unsubstantiated. The real parties, nameless as they still are, must have been discreet, the escapades indeed slight and few.

Two years after Bellini's death Heinrich Heine, who had known him slightly in Paris, brought out a masterpiece of perfidy, worthy both of a great poet and of an ancestor of popular journalism. Even in an age less sexually obsessed than ours it cannot have failed to call up a picture of effeminacy. Heine pretended to have been asked whether Bellini was good-looking, and answered that he was 'not ugly':

> He was a tall slender figure that moved in a graceful, I might say coquettish way; always finically dressed; face regular, long, rosy; hair light blond, almost golden, lightly curled; forehead noble, high, very high; nose straight; eyes pale blue; mouth well cut; chin round. His features had about them something vague and characterless, rather like milk, and this milky face sometimes curdled into a sweet-sour look of sadness. This sad look on Bellini's face made up for its want of spirit; but it was a sadness without depth; it glimmered without poetry in his eyes, it quivered without passion about his lips. The young maestro seemed to wish to make this shallow, languid sadness visible in his whole appearance. His hair was dressed in such a romantically wistful

fashion; his clothes fitted his frail body so languorously, and he carried his little malacca cane in such an idyllic manner, that he always reminded me of the young shepherds in our pastoral plays mincing about with beribboned crooks, in pastel jackets and breeches. And his gait was so maidenly, so elegiac, so ethereal. The creature altogether looked like a sigh in dancing pumps.

Rather than description, this was assassination by a poet 'satanically' inclined. Princess Belgiojoso, however – the Italian exile in whose salon Heine had met Bellini – more naively recalled Bellini's shape as 'rounded, effeminate, though most elegant. His whole person was in harmony with his tender and dreamy compositions.'

How much of this came of the general fixation on Bellini as 'elegiac' artist? Possibly a lot. Bellini's authentic letters are far from dreamy or languid; so is much of his work. But Belgiojoso (who, like another Paris hostess, called him 'childish') may have caught a wavering sexual identity. He told her that he disliked taking the initiative in love ('attacking a brand-new heart': it was like breaking in a horse or a pair of new boots) and hated still more the role of seducer: 'I want each to come half way.' Measured not against a 1990s ideal of men and women as equals, but against 1830s values that (as other evidence shows) Bellini took for granted, this marks some uncertainty. To Florimo he wrote of how susceptible he was, but also how quick to fall out of love. Perhaps he needed a warm, unquestioning love verging on the maternal. That would explain some of the problems with Turina.

Bellini's fear that his susceptibility might land him in a hazardous marriage, and his view of an affair with a married woman as a lightning-rod, have brought scorn from some modern writers. Balzac's novels remind us that in the early nineteenth century bourgeois marriage was in the first place a transaction over property and the future of the family; for a rising young man to put it off, and meanwhile enjoy a character-forming affair with a married woman, was normal. Bellini in this was normal; he just wrote about it more frankly than most.

The second letter Florimo printed has become famous. Bellini again wrote that he needed 'sentiment' and had quickly tired of mere sensual affairs. He told of his first meetings with Turina in Genoa; she had been unwell, he had spent days in her room, they had declared their love and spent hours kissing and embracing, but neither was sure of the other's constancy. Back in Milan came misunderstandings, coldnesses, explanations, absences:

> . . . the following week she was again in Milan, where, so as to stay with me, she seldom went to the theatre, and after many evenings of loving speeches, and embraces, and kisses, I plucked the flower of love almost in passing, for her father was in the house, and there we were with all the doors open: she in the ecstasy of love said: Bellini, will you always love me? will you love me still more? I swore that I would, I would love her if she always deserved it . . .

This rich, beautiful, attractive woman, previously so sociable – he reported – now wanted nothing so much as to be with him alone: 'all the signs are that she truly loves me, my mind is at peace, and it seems the affair is serious . . .' He ended by repeating that, apt as he was to fall madly in love, 'this love will save me from some marriage or other' (27 September 1828).

For the next few years a routine set in. Bellini became a friend of both the Turina and Cantù families, saw them in Milan, and spent part of the summer at one or other villa on the lake; he occasionally visited the Turina home at Casalbuttano. Until 1832 Giuditta did not accompany him on his trips away from Milan; appearances were kept up and Bellini wrote letters both to her and to her relatives, clearly meant to be passed round, in which he seemed a mere friend; he sometimes asked to be remembered to 'the good' or 'the impassible' Ferdinando Turina. On the other hand he wrote openly to certain friends, such as Pasta's husband, that 'Giuditta Turina and I' were spending time together; once, perhaps by a slip, he wrote her name 'Signora Bellini'.

The situation is clear – a common one in Italian upper- and middle-class families down to the 1950s. Giuditta, married at sixteen, had not hit it off with Ferdinando; divorce was impossible; the couple agreed, perhaps tacitly, to live and let live; Ferdinando allowed his wife to travel with her brother and spend time away from him; he tolerated Bellini; he, the two families, and everyone else knew or guessed what was going on, but they turned a blind eye so long as nothing happened to force a plain statement, a confrontation, or a scandal. If something did happen the delicate balance would be upset.

Not that all was plain sailing. Turina was subject to gynaecological ills that brought intense menstrual pains and laid her up for weeks. At least once (March 1829) she suffered from what appears to have been bulimia – over-eating followed by vomiting. This suggests tensions we have no means of gauging. The affair must at times have been, in Bellini's terms, more 'sentiment' than 'sensuality'.

He for his part had reservations. Before Florimo could respond to news of the affair he had written to soothe any possible upset: 'I am incredibly calm . . . I still have my career at heart . . . everything [else] is secondary when it's a question of losing both honour and fame' (5 October 1828). This determination to put his career first – a refrain throughout Bellini's short adult life – did not pass Turina by: she had asked, when they were still at the kissing stage, whether it might not take him away from her. As the affair took its course she had reason to feel unsure of her lover, whether she admitted it or not.

Meanwhile Bellini's career was steaming ahead. In spring 1828 he had offers from Turin, Venice, and Naples, but ended by signing on 16 June a contract for another opera at La Scala, this time to open the fashionable carnival season on 26 December. It meant – he was aware – running a risk from the expectations the Milan audience would have after *Pirata*.

In the event *La straniera* was an even wilder success. Bellini and Romani settled in early August on a French gothic novel by the Vicomte d'Arlincourt, set in a fancied medieval Britanny. Problems arose. Romani as usual was late, then seriously ill, then late again. The first performance was put off (to 14 February 1829), but at the New Year Romani went off to Venice on another job, leaving Bellini to take rehearsals – a task usually performed by the librettist. Opera being an affair of state, the government at first undertook to drag

8   Felice Romani, librettist of all but one of Bellini's mature operas.

Romani back, but he made out that he had no formal contractual obligation. Bellini was, as always, keen to get the best singers; he tried in vain to have Rubini transferred from Naples, thought for a moment of giving the lover's part to the baritone Tamburini, but was in the end pleasantly surprised by the tenor Domenico Reina. The prima donna on whom the title part was 'cut' was again Méric-Lalande; she was a brilliantly dramatic singer, though contemporaries have left us no adequate account.

La straniera is Bellini's most radical opera. It is at once the most violently romantic and the most severe in its shunning of ornament. Declamation, generally syllabic, leads into arioso that sounds like an incipient aria but refuses to develop into a closed form: Lippmann calls this 'the musicalization of recitative'. Solo arias are few; the tenor has none. Coloratura in the title part serves to introduce the strange lady offstage, and after that is wholly dramatic. The finale to the first half breaks up excitingly into short stammered phrases for the distraught heroine, with only one aria-like quatrain. All this bothered some critics, who wrote of 'sung declamation, or declaimed song', but the correspondent of the leading German music journal hailed Bellini's courage in 'bring[ing] opera back from its present slovenliness to the right path'; others praised his 'philosophical' music; all realized he had got clean away from the florid Rossinian style. Berlioz preferred La straniera among Bellini's works, no doubt because it came nearest to his own ideal.

Why is it so little known? It was a repertory work until about 1870. A basic problem is the story. Audiences can take a wild plot so long as emotions are clear: witness Il trovatore. In Straniera they might take the hero (Gualtiero was irrational, but Arturo is unhinged), they might take such a potentially ludicrous episode as tenor and baritone both falling or jumping into the lake only to re-emerge sensationally in the next act, if they could make out what stirs the heroine to continual despair. Alaide's problem is special indeed: she is the incognita ex-queen of France, repudiated but still in her own eyes the king's wife – hence another doomed Byronic outlaw, who can neither accept love nor reveal her secret. Bellini spotted at once the 'terrible difficulty' of expounding this; it was in fact impossible. Romani's two-page prefatory note was lost on one critic, who wrote that nobody could understand why Alaide and Arturo did not elope. Bellini, however, thought the 'situations' strong enough to carry the opera on their own. Most of the audience agreed. They roared their approval: it felt, Tamburini said, 'like a revolution'.

Little in *Straniera* is routine; nothing is languid. At worst, the barcarolle chorus that opens the first scene is a harmless pretext for a tableau, the stretta that closes it is tinny. Orchestral writing is as varied as in *Pirata*, with lovely woodwind introductions and an ostinato figure for lower strings, moody and tonally uncertain, that runs under Alaide's dialogue with her brother and brings a romantic sense of the unknown. Frequent modulations encode the instability that besets the characters. The composer's radicalism keeps enough of the normal structure of early nineteenth-century Italian opera to ensure a spare form, but cuts through it again and again for the sake of dramatic speed; a striking example is 'Che far vuoi tu?', in effect a dialogue trio (leading to a quartet) carried on wholly in arioso, over a simple, solemn accompaniment, but longer scenes too feel through-composed. Tamburini's gifts inspire a new kind of writing for baritone, a legato line at once honeyed and eloquent; the finest launches the trio 'No: non ti son rivale', admired by Verdi.

Best of all is Alaide's part. From the romanza, arioso, and duet that introduce her – the first impersonally lovely, the last an exquisite lament moving stepwise in small intervals – by way of much declamation to the 'long, long, long melody' and clamant energy of her double aria at the end, this is a part for a supremely versatile singing actress. If Maria Callas had sung it *La straniera* would now be on the map. Wagner, late in life, played themes from it among other Bellini works; with the regulation dig at the 'poverty' of such music, he said 'That is . . . real passion and feeling; all it needs to enchant people is for the right woman singer to come along and sing it.'

9   The great baritone Antonio Tamburini as Valdeburgo in *La straniera*.
Contemporary print.

3   The champion

An audience so enraptured that they yelled 'like mad people' and, in the second act, gave him an unheard of five curtain calls – that was the news Bellini sent his uncle after La straniera:

> . . . with God's help, I hope to stamp my name on the epoch . . . the public is kind enough to regard me as an innovative artist, and not as an imitator of Rossini's overwhelming art . . . tell everyone [in the family] that with this new opera my reputation is sky-high, and by unremitting application I hope to raise it higher still. I kiss your hands . . . (16 February 1829)

At twenty-seven, with only three professional operas to his name, Bellini felt sure of becoming champion.

In the cut-throat world of opera this was a position fixed by earning power; as a leading impresario put it, 'the price has to be the thermometer'. Within a month Bellini demanded, if he was to write another opera for La Scala, a fee of 10,000 francs – double the previous record fee, Rossini's 5,000 francs for Semiramide in 1823: 'If they want me, they'll have to pay me that, because I won't come down any further' (14 March 1829). Even after Pirata he had demanded a high fee to write an opera for London – negotiations fell through – and had set his sights on Paris, not just on mounting Pirata for the Théâtre-Italien but on composing, like Rossini, a French work for the Opéra.

Bellini's estimate of what he could achieve was realistic. He earned 10,000 francs for an opera within less than two years, and he won a contract for Paris within five. Each time, however, he had to experience a setback first. The failure of *Zaira* at the opening of the new Parma opera house (16 May 1829) was made up for by the success of *I Capuleti e i Montecchi* at La Fenice, Venice (11 March 1830). This in effect made Bellini champion – witness the fees he earned with *La sonnambula* (Milan, Teatro Carcano, 6 March 1831) and *Norma* (La Scala, 26 December 1831), followed by the enduring triumph of both works, each a pillar of the nineteenth-century repertoire. Then the initial failure of *Beatrice di Tenda* (La Fenice, Venice, 16 March 1833) ran ahead of a new departure and another triumph with the Paris work *I puritani*.

Though Bellini proved right, he had taken chances. In an art form made up of so many strands a lot could go wrong. Bellini was distinctive not just in his self-confidence but in his resolve. He meant to win on his own terms. He worked more slowly than his competitors, and he held out for exceptional rewards, even at the cost of being unemployed during the busy carnival season – something the folklore of the profession regarded as the worst possible advertisement; only luck fended this off in carnival 1830.

'Idleness bores me, taking risks makes me anxious, I dislike spending a long time without composing', he told Florimo – but he still would not write for what he considered a poor company of singers or an inadequate fee (9 June 1828). He tried to prevent Rubini's wife, to his mind a poor singer, from being cast in *Pirata* at Naples – he thought she would ruin the work – and got into a quarrel with the impresario Barbaja. To give way on such points, he wrote later, would suit neither his financial interests nor 'the decorum of my career' (19 September 1831).

Naively, as it seemed, Bellini explained that he had to charge high fees because he was a slow worker: 'I spend as much time on each [opera] as my fellow-composers do on three or four' (14 February 1834). His true stance was far from naive; nor was it at all like that of a traditional craftsman who worked slowly because he held to guild

practices. He knew the rules of the market. Barbaja grumbled that
Bellini had made him pay a high fee for Straniera, knowing him to be
badly in want of a new opera: Bellini replied that if his next opera was
a hit Barbaja would have to pay twice as much. The impresario, he
told Florimo, 'will be my friend as long as I do well'; only failure
would put him off (23 June, 6 August 1828). The assessment was as
accurate for the Italian opera world as it would have been later in
Hollywood.

Bellini was in fact a conscious modern artist who thought he
should be highly regarded and well paid so long as he delivered the
goods. Composers in his day often adapted their works for new
singers or new theatres, adjusting existing arias or writing new ones,
but Bellini disliked such tasks; once he had made a name he sought
to avoid them by holding out for an extravagantly high fee – a 'stop-
per'. Nor would he think of letting his fee for a new opera drop below
championship level: 'I will never come down from the prices I have
achieved', he wrote (18 October 1833), 'even at the cost of becoming
cathedral organist and composer in some other Novara' – an allusion to the gaunt northern town where his less successful colleague
Mercadante had become just that. Several composers took to church
music when opera turned sour; Bellini clearly regarded it as professional death.

A champion has to beat all comers. Much has been made of Bellini's 'paranoid' distrust of rival composers. He did conclude that
'friendship within the profession is quite impossible' (5 April 1828); he
did in the end automatically write down 'Donizetti's friends' as 'my
enemies' (27 February 1835); he did suspect or denounce intrigues
against him. Bellini undoubtedly saw the opera business as a tennis
court where you had to win or go under. But was he wrong? His attitude was in part justified, in part the common coin of the profession.

Among contemporaries his obvious rivals were Pacini and
Donizetti. By the time of his breakthrough with Pirata he was sure
that Pacini was intriguing against him in Milan (and Florimo in his
biography suggested that Pacini had already done so at Naples over

Bianca e Fernando). He may well have been right. Pacini was a manipulator of what we would call public relations; at least once he prearranged a 'spontaneous' torchlight procession of well-wishers after a first night. At La Scala his mistress, a Russian countess, was the centre of much gossip and faction. The manoeuvres of such factions cannot now be checked, but contemporary press comment shows that Bellini did not make them up; something was going on.[8]

Towards Donizetti the slightly younger Bellini was at first well disposed. In 1826–8 he sent him greetings and congratulations on a successful opera, told Florimo that he hoped for the success of another, and praised some of its music; though Donizetti occasioned the remark about the impossibility of friendship within the profession (by giving Bellini's leading soprano what seemed to be bad advice) Bellini still thought he had acted without malice. Donizetti's transformation into an 'enemy' came in 1830 with the success of his *Anna Bolena*: because it marked a new departure and lifted him into a higher class it made him a rival to be feared. From then on Bellini saw each of his own operas as a reply to Donizetti's last: volleys at match point.

Bellini's hostility to his fellow-composers, freely expressed in letters to Florimo, is much the same as Mozart's in his letters to his father; Mozart too suspected plots, not always without cause. Something like it is the attitude of many creative artists, taken up as they are with their own vision and needs: a rival's work easily becomes an obstruction or a threat. Donizetti – it is true – was generous to his fellows, but he, not Bellini, was the exception.

Nor should we be overimpressed with the language of 'enmity'. The opera market worked in a continual rush, intensified by bad roads and slow posts, and amid constant competition. Tempers frayed. Terms such as 'scoundrel', 'donkey', 'vile', etc., applied by Bellini to this or that member of the opera business (as a rule when that person had just acted unhelpfully in some specific matter), can be matched in the correspondence of many others; they do not mean what they would mean if uttered in a university committee.

From time to time Bellini wrote down what appears to be a general statement of his philosophy or his feelings about life. On a closer look this too turns out to have been a bromide or an immediate response to a spot of trouble. 'Self-love is innate in men' meant that he was staying on in Genoa to enjoy the triumph of *Bianca e Fernando*, 'the world is evil and full of selfishness' that people in Naples were blaming him for telling the truth about a poor singer, 'my life so far has been made up of nothing but trouble' that Florimo was unreasonably blaming him for not having helped a friend (19 April, 14 July, August 1828). On the evidence of his letters Bellini seems a fairly ordinary young southerner on the make, conventional in his notions of honour, his attitude to women, and his loyalty to the family, a trifle vain but not unpleasantly so; if he was egocentric it was as an artist determined to forward and protect his work in a tough market. Where did the pure, poignant feeling and the aristocratic distinction of his finest music come from? We do not know.

Bellini's contract for *Zaira*, signed in November 1828, antedated the triumph of *Straniera*. The opening of the new Parma opera house was a special occasion in more than one sense. The theatre belonged to the ruler (Napoleon's ex-empress Marie-Louise, awarded the duchy as consolation); nothing, down to the rise of the curtain, happened without her leave. It also focused the daily life and gossip of the upper classes: to keep them contented, the government sought a high standard of performance at low prices. Audiences took pride in Parma's status as capital and were notoriously hard to please.

Bellini therefore took a risk when he turned down a classical libretto by the Parma censor (the pompous official he so alienated with romantic talk of forests and tombs): the proposed subject, Caesar and Cleopatra, was – he said – 'old as Noah', and he persuaded the government to commission a new one from Romani instead. The official felt humiliated by 'vile and low people'; he was not without friends in Parma. Bellini thought he would have three months to compose the opera, but because Romani was working out of town a month went by before they agreed the subject (it was Bellini's idea to use Voltaire's tragedy *Zaïre*). Then Romani's lateness meant that, with under a month to go to the first night, part of the libretto was still missing; in a foreword unlikely to endear him to the Parmesans he half boasted, half apologized that he had had to write it 'in bits'. Bellini had to compose the music in about a month, something he later said was always damaging to him, short of a miracle. No miracle occurred to save *Zaira* from failure; the cause, however, seems to have been local resentment at the incomers rather than dislike of the work.

Zaira might have gone on to establish itself in other towns if luck had not intervened. Bellini had made up his mind to sit out the carnival of 1830 and wait till that of 1831, when he was due to write an opera for La Fenice, Venice, at that time one of the three leading Italian opera houses; meanwhile he agreed to introduce himself and his work to the Venetians by – for once – refitting the part of Imogene in *Pirata* to the mezzo Giuditta Grisi. He was therefore in Venice in January 1830 when Pacini failed at the last moment to deliver the new opera he had promised. The management asked Bellini to step in and he agreed.

It meant once again composing an opera within little more than a month. To avoid a frantic rush he got permission to use Romani's five-year-old libretto on the subject of Romeo and Juliet, originally written for the composer Vaccai: it would allow him at once to satisfy Grisi as Romeo – mezzos still sang lovers' parts – and to recycle about a third of the *Zaira* music; in the event, eight numbers and some shorter passages went into the new work. *Capuleti* was an instant success and shortly went the rounds of Europe. *Zaira* therefore vanished after just one production away from Parma. It has been rediscovered, mainly on records, in our own day.

Though *Zaira* and *Capuleti* were mutually exclusive at a time when most operas had to be new, they no longer are. Each has merits and drawbacks.

Capuleti is now one of the Bellini operas most often revived, in part because the story looks Shakespearian, in part because adept women singers are easier to find than a good Bellinian tenor and bass. The story, however, is not Shakespearian. Romani may not even have read Shakespeare; he went back to the Italian sources and to an earlier libretto. Romeo is a faction leader rather than an emblem of young love. Then the libretto, though Romani altered it, suffers here and there from having to be bent to pre-existing music, as in the odd emphasis given the word 'a' ('to') in Romeo's opening aria (on 'a lui diè morte') – a comedown from the stark declamation of La straniera. On the other hand the special glory of Capuleti, the tomb scene, much of it noble recitative or arioso to the barest accompaniment or none, was too bare for contemporary audiences; they quickly took to its replacement by Vaccai's conventional last scene, or a varying mixture of Vaccai and Bellini. Now that it is generally praised it needs, and seldom gets, a Romeo who can shape the Italian words and audiences that can follow them. Failing those, the scene (and the work as a whole) risks monotony.

Zaira has the more varied and exciting plot, a conflict of love and duty heightened by the oriental setting and by Voltaire's even-handed distribution of sympathy between the Christian slave girl and her Othello-like sultan lover. Its four principals (against three in Capuleti) also allow a more varied musical structure. Unfortunately the hurried timetable shows in weak patches; the least adequate, the big Act 1 finale, follows a commonplace tune with a stretta that is blatant without being effective.

Both works display – and in part share – an outpouring of melody more decorative than Bellini had allowed himself in La straniera. Zaira's opening aria starts with a Rossinian fountain of coloratura. The opera is like Semiramide in its oriental subject and its casting (soprano, contralto in breeches, bass weighty but elegant, subsidiary tenor and second bass). That may have inspired not only such ornate moments (with an added Bellinian distinction, morbidezza, tenderness) but the well-articulated ensemble in Act 1 that begins with a duet for contralto and bass and turns into a quintet: like the finest scenes in Rossini's opera, it effectively moves the action forward

10 Maria Malibran as Romeo in *I Capuleti e i Montecchi*. Contemporary miniature.

while achieving a warm sonority. None of this went into *Capuleti*, but Bellini did re-use the last part of the soprano-contralto duet, another scene inspired by *Semiramide*; a characteristic Bellinian melody, undulant, turning round and round on itself, beautifully fitted to the words, achieves a sense of ecstasy through saturation in music.

How conscious was Bellini's move away from the austerity of *La straniera*? When asked about his motives as a composer, he was apt to deny that he had been influenced, for instance by Rossini, and to say that he had 'written music such as the feelings of my heart dictated'. We may think, all the same, that he took note of the criticisms aimed at *La straniera* (even though they did not keep it from successfully doing the rounds of the theatres). For Italian audiences the work's declamatory, proto-Wagnerian aspect was best taken in small doses. There are still splendid recitatives and ariosos in both *Zaira* and *Capuleti*: not only Romeo's tomb scene but several for him and, in *Zaira*, for both the heroine and the bass: noble, dignified, pathetic. The balance of these operas, however, tilts towards arias and closed forms, themselves less bound to syllabic utterance of the words. Nor would the subjects of Bellini's operas ever again match the frenzy of *Pirata* or *Straniera*. After the initial impact of romanticism a tendency reasserted itself – normal among Italians of the time – to frame the new heightened emotions in classical language and elegant musical setting.

Where *Zaira* and *Capuleti* showed a continuing weakness was in fast passages, cabalettas in particular. Some were little better than routine. One, already effective, was much improved when transferred to *Capuleti* (and from minor to major) as 'La tremenda ultrice spada', Romeo's defiance at the end of his opening aria; its wide leaps and martial gait are genuinely heroic, far removed from 'languor'. *Capuleti* also has a notable edge in the finale to the first half, in part taken from the trio in *Zaira*. It opens, to an anxious descending string phrase over a steady beat, with a series of arioso fragments for Juliet ('Tace il fragor'), shortly joined by Romeo. All this is in Bellini's radical declamatory manner; it sounds improvised and spontaneous. Then, with everyone on stage, both the slow quintet, a cappella to begin with ('Soccorso, sostegno') and the fast section it resolves itself into ('Se ogni speme') set off Romeo and Juliet musically against the opposed Capulets and Montagues; in the latter part the lovers' melody flings a great arc over the syllabic defiance of the rest. Bellini here showed himself able to build an operatic structure on a large scale.

Not without cost to himself. The penetrating Venetian winter gave him a bad cold, and the effort of writing *Capuleti* ten hours a day with another four-hour spell at night upset his digestion. This was no doubt why, back in Milan in April, he suffered loss of appetite and, on 21 May, a sudden 'bilious gastric inflammatory fever' from which it took him more than a month to recover, perhaps less through bleeding and emetics than through Marianna and Francesco Pollini's devoted care. Without that, he thought, the illness might have been his last.

It was almost certainly the amoebic dysentery that was indeed to kill him five years later. He had had unspecified ill health in 1828 and was to have a brief 'gastric' recurrence in 1834, each time in hot weather. Amoeba infection or amoebiasis was until recently common in the hotter parts of Europe; it still is endemic in tropical regions such as south-east Asia. There, people with amoebas in their digestive system may not be ill, especially if a high-bulk, largely vegetarian diet keeps the parasites absorbed and prevents them from ulcerating the bowels or reaching the liver. This helps to explain the long periods in which Bellini's complaint seems not to have troubled him. In his day its cause was not understood; nor did doctors know how to treat it. Bellini himself held to such explanations as lack of air in his rooms, or a 'bad humour' in the blood. His belief in a senna-and-treacle laxative called 'Elixir du Roi' has been blamed for hastening his death, but he did counsel moderation in its use (whatever that may have meant), so one cannot be sure.

By 1 July 1830 he was convalescing on Lake Como. By the end of the month or the very beginning of August he had signed a contract with the impresario Giuseppe Crivelli (who then managed La Scala and La Fenice) for two operas. He had hoped to be paid 10,000 francs for each opera, but agreed to 10,000 Austrian lire (8,700 francs). In the event, a group of rich Milanese who had decided to mount a season at the Teatro Carcano in opposition to La Scala bought out Bellini's contract and made a new one: this one promised him 12,000 Austrian lire (10,440 francs) and half the rights in the score. With it he at once broke through the 10,000-franc barrier and established a new record; he was champion.

He had moved fast: for *Straniera* he had been paid 4,350 francs (double the fee for *Pirata*), for *Zaira* 5,000, for *Capuleti* 6,500 (more than Donizetti would earn for a major carnival opera at La Scala in 1833 and 1835). The time had now come to plan the rest of his career: how was he to make the most of the championship he had achieved?

In the early nineteenth century a lifelong career, with retirement at sixty or sixty-five, was by no means the ideal. Aristocratic notions of 'an independence' – wealth such as to free one from the need to earn – had not yet given way to the 'religion of work'. Those who followed an arduous profession hoped to reach that 'independence' quickly. In Britain, young men who went out to the East India Company's civil service looked to achieve it and go home within ten years or so. In the opera world, Giuditta Pasta at twenty-nine thought of retiring at thirty-two. Just after he had broken through in 1830, Bellini thought he might in four years accumulate enough capital not to have to work again. That need not have stopped him from composing; but he could then have done it at his own pace, like his rich contemporary Meyerbeer.

When Bellini hoped for 'an independence' he did not forget his family. His plan was to pay them an assured income of six Sicilian ounces (£4, or 100 francs) a month, which in Catania would go a long way. Meanwhile he was sending them 30 ounces (£20) and hoped to go on at the rate of £40 a year so long as he kept getting good contracts (1 July 1830).

Nor did he neglect the chance of starting a family of his own. In the summer of 1831 he thought of one day marrying Pasta's daughter Clelia, then thirteen; they had all been spending time on the lake, he and Pasta as colleagues were on excellent terms, Clelia's parents at any rate gave him the impression that they would consider the match, and Pasta's mother, an important member of the household, seems to have favoured it.[9] His affair with Turina, which the Pastas knew about, need not have stood in the way, especially if he was thinking some years ahead: it might by then be over, or he could bring it to what contemporaries would have thought a natural end.

Meanwhile Bellini as champion composer in the Italian opera league was a mixture of the sharp and the inexperienced. In some ways he was ill-equipped for financial dealings in relatively advanced Milan, let alone Paris. His early life in Sicily and Naples had left him with an understandable distrust of banks, he seems never to have grasped what a limited liability company might mean, and in the first flush of success with *Pirata* he wrote, perhaps only half jokingly, that he might invest his earnings in a 'fief' – still the Sicilian term for landed property (12 January, 20 February 1828). What he actually did with his money was to place it with somebody else: to begin with, Giuditta Turina. Some writers have been indignant at her having to pay him 5 per cent interest; this was, however, a normal transaction, often engaged in among themselves by members of upper-class families both in Italy and in Britain. No doubt she in turn invested the money, and was not out of pocket.

In his early days in Milan he lived carefully, eating at a restaurant only on Friday and Saturday, and having Florimo in Naples post letters on to Sicily to save fivepence. The rented rooms he lived in, there and, later, in Paris, were centrally located and well furnished but not large. The only luxury he indulged himself in seems to have been clothes. By 16 January 1828 he was asking Florimo to send him two dozen pairs of gloves – 'one can never have too many'. Well-dressed people wore gloves far more than they do now, but Bellini was undoubtedly a dandy. His wardrobe at his death was extensive.

Bellini lived in a time of transition when Italian composers witnessed more and more exploitation of their successful works, but could only get a share of the rewards with difficulty.

Eighteenth-century operas had by and large been new. The composer earned a flat fee; he could hope to recycle some of the music in another opera and another town; if a successful work was given again in smaller towns, without payment to him, the potential earnings thus lost did not amount to much. The lack of copyright in the Italian states was not then an issue.

Already in the last quarter of the century, with the expansion of the market, some operas circulated widely. Matters came to a head with the appearance, about 1810, of successful Italian music publishers. These depended largely on exploiting new operas through the sale of vocal scores and of arias adapted for all kinds of solo instruments; they also ran a copying business on the side. Money could now be made, both by hiring out the hand-copied orchestral score and parts to theatre managements and by selling printed music to amateurs. Bellini could therefore hope to earn something, not just from a flat fee but from selling or sharing the rights in the score and the publication rights; yet in the absence of copyright treaties among the Italian states (concluded only from 1840), he might in practice see hardly any return. The question was all the more acute for him because he depended on a few highly successful operas rather than on a fast turnover of new works.

The basic problem was that an impresario or a publisher might either steal an authentic score (as a rule by bribing a copyist) or pirate it by getting a minor composer to work up a new orchestral setting from the printed vocal score – not too difficult when orchestration was relatively thin; even if the outcome was crude it passed muster with some audiences. An impresario who wanted to give a recent opera would commonly try to knock down the cost of hiring the authentic score by pointing out that he could get one elsewhere at half the asking price. Not even a member of the august Milanese ducal house of Visconti, who had the management of La Scala from 1834, was above such tactics. Printed music too raised difficulties: a

Milan publisher who hoped to sell his output in Naples might find that a Naples publisher had got in first; sometimes a rival might beat him to the draw even in his own state.

To Bellini these conditions meant maximum annoyance for relatively little gain. He did sell the rights in his operas, under a variety of arrangements. Ownership of the full score he generally split with the impresario or with the Milan publisher Giovanni Ricordi, sometimes three ways with both; but according to Ricordi, the hiring out of so popular a work as Norma brought in little or nothing because 'all of Italy, all of Germany, all of Europe is flooded with [pirated] Normas'. Ricordi may have piled it on somewhat for his own bargaining purposes – he had in fact hired out the authentic score to five or six theatres; the difficulty was none the less real.

The right to publish the vocal score and extracts Bellini sold for a lump sum, but at a time when the Italian demand for printed music was still small this too was modest: for the right to print La sonnambula, together with one-third of the rights in the score, he got from Ricordi 4,000 Austrian lire (3,480 francs) – one-third of his flat fee for the opera. This was if anything a high-water mark: Bellini later demanded 3,500 Austrian lire (3,045 francs) for Beatrice di Tenda (publishing rights and half the rights in the score), and he let Ricordi have the publishing rights in Puritani for the Austrian states for 2,000 francs.[10] Only in France would he find a richer society, better able to pay and with an effective copyright law.

Meanwhile he tried to find ways of countering piracy or getting round it. Against pirated performances in the Two Sicilies, his own country, he several times called on the government and the police: let them either ban the performance or at least compel the management to state that the score had been worked up by Maestro So-and-So. There is no sign that anything came of this.

In 1832 he thought he might avoid all the trouble over piracy by selling the rights in his next opera at one go for just over 13,000 francs (he seems to have meant the rights in the full score, not the publishing rights). Two years later he devised a scheme for a three-year contract whereby all the leading managements in Italy and Germany would undertake to buy an authentic copy of each new Bellini opera for a modest fee of 500 francs, to safeguard it, and to use it only in their own theatres; a variant was for Ricordi to pay 4,000 francs for the rights in each opera, and for publisher or composer to give out the score and charge a fee according to which of them was approached first. The purpose of these arrangements was to squeeze out the pirates and get rid of the bewildering division of rights among the composer, the publisher, and the original impresario, which might require a three-cornered correspondence and easily brought about a muddle.

Bellini was casting about for a regular, dependable system that would both ensure him a legitimate reward and avoid continual bargaining – something Verdi was to achieve from 1847, but only because copyright had become enforceable. In Bellini's lifetime that resource was wanting; though his schemes again led nowhere, they did embody a modern search for efficiency and for enhanced professional standing.

Where piracy reigned, it was difficult to be always honest. Bellini engaged in a few transactions that were at least dubious. If he had been challenged, he might have said that his partners had done or would do the same to him; it would have been true.

A common ploy in the opera business was to exaggerate one's last fee in the hope of talking up the next. Bellini did this when he wrote to Florimo (in a letter meant to be shown to the impresario Barbaja, who might commission a new opera for Naples) that he had been paid for *La sonnambula* 15,000 Austrian lire plus half the rights; the sum he had in fact received was 12,000. This was something of a white lie: Bellini named the true figure to the noble superintendent of Naples theatres, explaining that he had no use for half the Naples rights (because he rightly judged that they would bring him in nothing unless he was on the spot) and therefore could not settle for less than 15,000 as a lump sum (19 September 1831). In dealing with Barbaja, a master bazaar bargainer, he clearly thought some finessing was needed.

At least once Bellini went behind the back of one publisher to make an illicit arrangement with another. He returned a favour from the Naples publisher Guillaume Cottrau by sending him the new big scene from the revised *Bianca e Fernando*, the exclusive rights to which he had split with Ricordi, and enjoined secrecy 'so as not to compromise my honour with my publisher here' (24 May 1828). He later countenanced a vocal score of *Straniera* pirated by the Milan publisher Ferdinando Artaria, even though he had sold the rights to Ricordi, and again enjoined secrecy. His motive was to ensure that the adaptation was 'as good as possible'; to this end he may even have supplied Artaria with a full score, though the evidence is not conclusive.[11] These were breaches of contract. It has to be said that Ricordi was as willing to pirate an opera as he was to denounce piracy at his expense, that Cottrau was just the same, that the Naples composer Carlo Conti, a fellow-student of Bellini's, offered to provide a stolen copy of a Rossini score, and that London and Paris managements were as ready as Italian to use pirated orchestral parts.[12] Bellini's conduct was not admirable, but it came of a gap in the law that almost enforced shady dealing.

In more straightforward business matters Bellini held his own. He twitted Ricordi when the publisher, as was his wont, cried poor: 'your letter . . . is so gloomy that if I did not know your business was flourishing I would fear a looming bankruptcy!' (20 March 1829). As a fledgling composer, with *Pirata* just behind him, he showed coolness in handling the shrewd and blustering Barbaja, at that time in charge of both the leading Italian opera houses. Barbaja was furious at Bellini's attempts to stop Rubini's wife from singing *Pirata* in Naples, and sent him an insulting letter. When the impresario came to Milan, Bellini, feeling 'irascible in the extreme', avoided him by dropping a visiting card when he knew Barbaja was out. The two then met by chance:

> Barbaja . . . with a smile shook my hand, greeting me in his usual style: 'You bloody fool, did you get my letter?' I answered coldly . . . that the opening words of his letter had made me feel sure that it

was not addressed to me, and I therefore tore it up . . . he . . . trying
to disguise his annoyance with a smile, said he would give me a
copy so that I could read it over every morning; but I, still as coldly
as could be, told him he could keep such letters for others, and that
Bellini was ashamed at the mere thought that a Barbaja could
suspect one who had ever been his grateful friend and who had
always, quite unselfishly and tactfully, asked for his just rights
and avoided intrigue . . . (9, 11 June 1828)

Bellini also persuaded the impresario that his suspicion of Florimo
had been unfounded. They then talked of other things; Barbaja invited Bellini to lunch the next day, and over the meal offered him the
contract that led to La straniera.

This is of course Bellini's account, but it rings true. By the standards of the Italian opera business the young composer had little
trouble in imposing himself; his unprecedented financial demands
were met, with only a minimum of bargaining – evidence that people
acknowledged his quality.

His artistic demands too were persuasive, if we are to believe an
account by an aristocratic friend of his, Count Barbò. He claimed to
have overheard from the next room a conversation during which
Bellini set out to make the tenor Rubini – an outstanding voice but,
until then, a stiff actor – show expression as the hero of Il pirata.
Barbò may have dressed it up a little, but again it rings true.

'You're cold and languid', Bellini said after he and the tenor had
rehearsed the duet; 'put a bit of passion into it: have you never been
in love?' He added: 'Dear Rubini . . . are you thinking about being
Rubini – or Gualtiero? . . . Don't you know that your voice is a gold
mine, not all of it yet discovered?' Mere vocal prowess was not
enough. Rubini answered that he could not make believe that he was
desperate and furious.

Confess (Bellini replied) that the real reason is you don't care for
my music, because it doesn't give you the usual opportunities; but
if I had taken it into my head to create a new genre and a musical
style that strictly expresses the words, and to make singing and

drama into an integral whole, ought I to give it up because you don't wish to support me? You can, all you need to do is forget yourself and throw yourself wholeheartedly into the character you're playing. Look . . .

Then, in a voice of no particular quality but with 'his face and his whole person animated', Bellini 'brought out singing so pathetic and moving that it clutched and tore at the heart'. After a while Rubini came in with his own voice and with the right feeling: the great romantic tenor had found himself.

Something like that was probably going on when, hearing Bellini talk to Giuditta Pasta as they came away from rehearsal, Lady Morgan thought he 'scolded his great pupil like a *petite pensionnaire* [little schoolgirl]'. Bellini may have been exerting a natural artistic authority, at odds with his dandyish looks.

In both his business and his artistic dealings he believed from the start in his own high gift, and acted on his belief. This was the period when Napoleon was only the mightiest example of a young man who had made his way by his own efforts. Bellini did not, like Julien Sorel in Stendhal's *Scarlet and Black*, have Napoleon consciously in mind, but he too pursued 'the career open to talent'. There was a price to pay in 'agitation' and ill health while he had an opera on the stocks, and in suspicion and anger at the (often all too genuine) bad behaviour of the opera world – though Verdi was to suffer worse tension during his 'years in the galleys'. Not even Verdi, however, was able to convince people as fast as Bellini did that his gift was indeed unique.

4   At the height of his powers

Women workers from the textile mills of Como would go back on Saturday evening to their home villages, singing folk songs as the boat crossed the lake. Bellini, himself adrift in a small boat, noted down the tunes; together with the surrounding hills and the vegetation that feathered the lake shore, these melodies inspired the idyll of *La sonnambula*.

Such at least was the account of one observer, a young girl growing up by the lake, who years afterwards would marry the ageing librettist Romani. It seems plausible: the villagers in *La sonnambula* do sing two choruses whose droning accompaniments allude to rather than directly represent north Italian folk music; at the climax, when the heroine sleepwalks past the millrace on to safe ground, the horns softly intone something like the alpine call (*ranz des vaches*) that in Rossini's *Guillaume Tell*, a year and a half earlier, had blessed the wider liberation of the Swiss.[13] Though the text mentions Switzerland, and the original production ran to peaks and fir trees, *La sonnambula* in spirit belongs to the region where alpine and Mediterranean cultures meet beside the lake.

Bellini, still recovering at first from his severe bout of dysentery, spent July and August on Lake Como, but for a fortnight or so was in the crushing heat of Bergamo: *La straniera* did well in the city's important trade fair season. That apart, he was on holiday and did not compose: he disliked working in the heat and planned a September start on his next opera, back in Milan.

By 15 July he and Romani had chosen to adapt Victor Hugo's ultra-romantic drama *Hernani*, which had opened in Paris only a few months earlier to scandal and riot; according to a letter published (and perhaps altered) by Florimo, he liked the subject 'very much' and so did Giuditta Pasta, the great singer who was to appear in one of his works for the first time.

On the lake he had been seeing a good deal of Pasta as well as living – discreetly – with his own Giuditta and her family. Pasta was to be the heroine of his next three operas and the making of his two undoubted masterpieces, *La sonnambula* and *Norma*. At a time when a new opera was moulded to the singers her artistic capacities were vital to what Bellini could hope to achieve.

Those capacities were very wide. Contemporaries acknowledged in her a 'sublime' tragedian who could be as effective in comic opera and who was mistress of coloratura. Above all, she could distil pathos into classical simplicity and grandeur. Changing fashions in acting style apart, her art had much in common with that of Maria Callas, down to the technical vocal difficulties both of them faced; Pasta's trouble – manifest just after her three Bellini creations – was that she sometimes sang uncontrollably out of tune.

To Bellini she and her family were already friends; after Pasta and he had worked together to establish his finest operas she became an 'angel' towards whom he felt 'grateful adoration that will end only with my life' – a real and understandable feeling.

Versatile though Pasta was, she liked – and, as an exceptional artist, was able – to concentrate on a few parts that suited her. Four of these, widely unalike, suggested what she could do with the parts Bellini had in mind for her. As Rossini's Tancredi, a crusader-lover, and as Romeo in Zingarelli's opera, she had brought off male parts no less demanding than the bandit hero Hernani was likely to be. Her Nina, the girl driven mad for love in Paisiello's opera, was a model Bellini consciously used for *La sonnambula*; its distinguishing mark was pathos reached through utmost simplicity of means. Mayr's Medea and Rossini's Semiramide stood behind the tragic heroine Norma.

11 Giuditta Pasta and G. B. Rubini, the original leads in *La sonnambula*. The hero's vaguely seventeenth-century costume is not called for by the libretto, but historical costume was generally required in opera.

Over *Ernani* – the Italian spelling of the work – Romani was as usual late because he had taken on too much: Bellini wrote on 17 November that he had been able to compose nothing for lack of words. He must, however, have written his usual wordless sketches (two went into *Sonnambula*), and at some time, probably that same month, he wrote fragments to texts in which a king of Spain appears – not always the same one. This points to the difficulties with the censorship that shortly led Romani (as Bellini reported on 3 January 1831) to give up the project for fear of 'compromising himself', that is, of risking serious delay.

Was this the whole story? Verdi was to get *Ernani* past a later Habsburg official. The Lombardo-Venetian censors were, before 1848, the most reasonable in Italy; they were apt to demand changes, not necessarily thoroughgoing, rather than to forbid a subject outright. The chief stumbling-blocks in Hugo's drama were a clamant suicide – religion and morality at that time bothered the censor more than politics – and a plot to kill a ruling monarch, foiled, however, by the ruler's courage and magnanimity. These might have been got through, or got round, though at the cost of losing valuable time. Bellini, some have suggested, may have come to dislike the wild romanticism *Hernani* stood for, or he may have wished to mark off his opera from Donizetti's *Anna Bolena*, which was to open the carnival season with Pasta in the lead. Pasta herself may have wished to avoid appearing in one sombre melodrama after another. This is all speculation: the latter half of 1830 is one of the periods in Bellini's life we know least about. We do know that the subject he and Romani settled on, in late November or early December, was in strong contrast to *Anna Bolena* with its prolonged mad scene and impending execution.

Sleepwalking none the less tapped the romantic interest in the unconscious and the strange. In *La sonnambula* it hints at a shadow side to the outwardly calm village life, even though it leads to nothing worse than a temporary misunderstanding as the innocent young bride Amina walks into the count's hotel bedroom. The subject came from a Paris narrative ballet, three years old; ballet and opera did at that time borrow plots from one another. Only on 2 January could Bellini start composing, with, as he thought, seven weeks to go to the first night on 20 February, but on 7 February he was still waiting for the text of Act 2; the opera was first performed on 6 March, to great acclaim. He later thought his having brought it off in six or seven weeks was 'a fluke': by rights, given his need to work slowly, it should have flopped.

Something else we do not know is who chose to alter the original story, shifting it from Provence to Switzerland and doing away with the count's recognition of the orphan Amina as his illegitimate daughter – a cut made so hastily that in the final version the count still sees in Amina's features an unexplained likeness. Bellini, most people have supposed, demanded these changes to bring out the innocence of the characters and remove any traces of boulevard piquancy. It seems likely. The libretto allowed for piquancy, not just in the deleted passages; it showed the count as a bit of a pompous ass and the villagers as well-meaning simpletons. Its situations also lent themselves to parody, above all the heroine's sleepwalking perilously along the eaves of the mill roof to the consternation of everyone else (her crossing a rotten bridge over the millrace was a variant devised some years after the first performance). Bellini magicked away all these potentially comic elements. In the words of Francesco Degrada, he 'dealt with the story . . . in a mood of extreme inwardness and of profound, total seriousness and emotional concentration'; he made a gimcrack theatrical world at once authentic and ideal.

What the music establishes – so Degrada argues in his most perceptive commentary – is neither a real village nor a pastoral convention; it is, as in the poetry of Leopardi (or, we might add, of John Clare), a 'dream landscape of the soul', where the characters are 'complementary aspects of a melancholy yearning for a lost world' of rural innocence and purity; such a world can spring back to life only through the illusion of art. The relation between Amina and Elvino in particular is 'an intense and pure bond between souls, in which ancestral values live again typical of an utterly southern, Catholic tradition: the poetry of marriage, of the family, a tender piety towards the dead whose mute presence hovers in benediction over the living[; this] steeps the two figures in an atmosphere we may well call religious'. The 'religion' invoked is that of feeling and of a 'fraternal participation' of the spiritual world in the life of human beings and of nature.

Nothing better illustrates this tone of grave simplicity, charged with feeling, than Elvino's arrival to sign the marriage contract. Amina's innocence has been established by her opening aria and the villagers' $\frac{6}{8}$ chorus with its rotating, folk-dance-like movement, the section for women's voices alone a distillation of rural freshness. First a little skittering phrase marks the arrival of the notary, then six modulating minim chords, pianissimo, as Elvino walks on, bring a rapt expectancy.[14] His recitative follows, animated and soaring to a gentle B flat. He is late because he has gone to ask 'an angel's blessing on our vows':

> . . .prostrate at my mother's tomb, 'Oh! bless
> My betrothed' I begged, 'she has
> All your virtues: let her make
> Your son as happy as you made
> His father.' I hope, my beloved,
> My mother heard me.

To the notary's questions Elvino replies that he brings to the marriage 'my farms, my house, my name, all I possess'; Amina, 'only my heart'. The words seem to come off an early Victorian sampler; yet the music, at once plain and laden with feeling, betrays not a touch of complacency or excess. It breathes sentiment, not sentimentality.

There follows the duet 'Prendi, l'anel ti dono', a long $\frac{12}{8}$ andante sostenuto in A flat, undulating forward by small steps mostly of a tone or semitone, into which Amina breaks with her F minor allegretto section 'Ah vorrei trovar parole', a shaded, downward trickling Chopin mazurka slightly before its time. Here is the music of love calm and assured, flecked with anguish at excess of happiness;

the final section ('Tutto, ah! tutto in questo istante') bursts into more commonplace joy. Bellini's gaze, at once trusting and exact, deals in emotions basic to humanity. Much Victorian art was to overdo them no less readily than the art of our own day hastens to spurn them, dedicated as much of it is to the knowing and the extreme.

The voice rules *La sonnambula* as it does not quite rule Bellini's earlier works. It is exposed, sometimes left unaccompanied, for the most part lightly sustained. It takes off in coloratura flights undreamt of in *La straniera*. Not that decoration is mere artifice. Giuditta Pasta, for whom the opera was written, could be an eagle or a dove; she was never a canary.

Amina's opening recitative and double aria ('Come per me sereno'), a song of joy on the day of her betrothal, touches its sinuous line with *fioriture* aptly called by Herbert Weinstock 'natural exhalations' of the girl's trust in love. The cabaletta ('Sovra il sen la man mi posa') brings a twenty-note descending scale and bursts of staccato decoration that can, according to the singer's dramatic commitment, suggest an ecstasy of delight or a marvellously iced cake; there is no doubt about which is intended. (These alternative effects are well shown in the recordings by Callas and Sutherland.) The lovers' second duet, born of jealous misunderstanding to end in harmony ('Son geloso del zeffiro errante'), 'seems' – a review of the first performance said – 'a competition in trills, scales, and roulades, but it is a great thing of its kind'. The lovers' trills and wave-like melismata, lovely in themselves, die down; the duet, already shaded by a characteristic excursion into the minor, ends in falling melodies that bring a sense of purity steadily deepened, till the lovers exchange the quiet folk-like refrain 'Even in sleep my heart will see you.' Vocal display is at every point a carrier of feeling.

The prime example of what Bellini could now do with the voice is the celebrated aria ('Ah non credea mirarti') in which Amina, still sleepwalking, looks at the flowers Elvino gave her and recalls her desolate state. Here is the type of the 'long, long, long melodies' admired by Verdi, 'such as no one before him had ever written'. In contrast with Bellini's usual scheme of short sections repeated and modified ($a^1a^2ba^2$), the plangent A minor melody wanders without repeating itself through eleven bars; Elvino's brief interjection ('I can no longer bear it') then continues it, but in the relative major, while Amina pulls back towards the minor; even when she moves for a time into C major, the woodwinds' cunningly timed interventions avoid a full cadence, and the melodic span moves, as it seems, unbroken to its final wordless lament. After Amina wakes and the lovers make it up, the cabaletta ('Ah! non giunge uman pensiero') need only be a leaping exultation.

Elvino's aria of despair ('Tutto è sciolto') in its briefer way is as intense. The count's aria ('Vi ravviso, o luoghi ameni') has been called Verdian, but it is Verdi's baritone arias (such as 'Il balen del suo sorriso' in *Trovatore*) that hark back to Bellini's with their legato at once mellifluous and stringent. Of the two arias for Lisa the innkeeper, one is agreeable, the other brilliant, neither is memorable; they suit her role as Amina's opposite and foe. *Sonnambula* has no lapses.

Bellini knitted the chorus into the action more closely than was usual in Italian opera, and he worked out to the limit his new, spare orchestration.

The choruses are just what the situations call for: not showy but apt. The music neither guys the villagers nor builds them up. As they evoke the supposed ghost that has been seen walking about, the mood they establish, to quiet horns and pizzicato strings, is of mild anxiety within the idyll; the opening chorus of Act 2, gentle $\frac{3}{4}$ musing followed by resolution, shows a group of limited but humane people doing their best. Hints of bagpipe music mark their change of mood, as they preceded the account of the ghost, and tell us the kind of ideal peasants these are. The chorus (men and women differentiated) back syllabically the slow section of the Act 1 finale: a great swinging $\frac{12}{8}$ melody expands from Elvino's solo to a quintet for the principals, in which voices fall and rise like the waves of the sea, time suspended; as this hugely effective piece unfolds the villagers are the community whose looking on brings Amina's shame.

By cutting down the orchestration to a minimum Bellini earned black marks that have followed him ever since. This happened first in France, together with Germany the home of orchestral music in his day. He was, Berlioz wrote in his obituary, 'unskilled at large-scale musical organization, little versed in the science of harmony, and virtually ignorant of instrumentation', altogether a 'second-rate musician' though with some 'naive' virtues. Rossini, by then in effect a French composer, used more discreet language in his comments and in his suggestions to Bellini's French biographer Pougin, but their purport was much the same. By the late nineteenth century the 'poverty' of Bellini's orchestration was a matter of course for musicians like Wagner and Verdi who admired him on other grounds.

Even then a few maintained that Bellini's procedures were both conscious and right. The composer Ferdinand Hiller, who had known him in Paris, wrote in a perceptive though at times inconsistent memoir that his orchestration might not sound much, 'but he knew very well what he wanted, and was far removed from the naive artist [*Naturdichter*] many have represented him as'. He was sparing with 'piquant' harmony – Hiller pointed to 'Ah vorrei trovar parole' in the first *Sonnambula* duet, where a poignant shading comes through two modulations in the accompanying chords to two half-measures – but what he did do in this line, along with much else in his work, testified to 'acute perception, warm feeling, and total mastery of means'. Another contemporary German composer, J. C. Lobe, dismissed talk of Bellini's 'ignorance' and commended his bare orchestral writing as designed to bring out the vocal line, though he too saw 'poverty' in the purely instrumental writing of overtures and transitional movements. It was left to the Italian composer Ildebrando Pizzetti, in a noted essay first published in 1915, to judge that what others called 'poverty' came of 'voluntary renunciations imposed by a sensibility of extraordinary delicacy and purity'.

Bellini himself wrote, in reply to a notion of Florimo's that he should reorchestrate *Norma* to meet French taste: 'You are mistaken: here and there it might work, but in general I would find it impossible because of the plain and flowing nature of the melodies, which admit no other kind of instrumentation than what is there already: and this I have fully thought through' (13 August 1835). Wagner, when he tried to do the job, reached the same conclusion. In recent years Bellini's view has come to be shared more widely, though the old clichés are not spent.

Sonnambula is full of orchestral effects that move the drama forward, but so deliberately plain and fined down that they may escape ears steeped in late romantic music. Just three modulating chords, spaced out, bring Amina past the spot over the millrace that nearly gives way under her, and down to safety; no more is needed. Horns, the romantic instrument, take over at that point; they accompany several other important passages and bathe the opera in a mood of recollection and distance, always tactfully. Briefest mode or key changes mark a shift of feeling, as when a D major chord in the E flat major 'ghost' chorus lets the ghost pass by. Even repeated pizzicato chords or arpeggio figurations have a charm of their own, often because their rhythms are unobtrusively delicate and right; the young Wagner (writing about *Norma*) thought the 'solid, regular periodic structure' of the orchestral accompaniment under the flowing vocal line made for a subtle dialectic of movement and stasis, and lifted Italian opera out of routine.

Modern audiences can hear all this, but only if the conductor and the players believe in the work; flinging on *La sonnambula* as a sop to bel canto fanciers will not do. Gravely simple, intimately tough, the opera sits at an angle to the present age, which finds innocence a stumbling-block; it may even strike some as ridiculous. In time, however, the laugh will not be on it.

Again we know little of Bellini's everyday life in the months between the triumph of *La sonnambula* in March 1831 and the first night of *Norma* on 26 December. As before, he spent most of July and August on Lake Como; this was when he began to think of one day marrying Pasta's daughter, without – it seems – as yet impairing his relationship with Turina. His work on *Norma* apart, all we know is that he denounced pirates of the Sonnambula score and thought of a possible opera for Naples.

For the moment, however, Milan kept him busy. From April at least he had known that he would write the opening work of the carnival season at La Scala, with Pasta and the robust tenor Domenico Donzelli in the leads, and by 27 July he knew the subject; Romani, he said, had chosen it (they may well have chosen it together) to fit Pasta's 'encyclopaedic character' – her prodigious versatility as both singer and actress. By a piece of luck Romani was for once on time: he provided the first scene on 31 August. Bellini, back in Milan, got down to work early in September; he had three months to complete the opera by the first rehearsal, probably on 5 December, and he seems to have got an unusual sense of calm from a cholera epidemic, then in Vienna, that seemed likely to reach Milan and close the theatres.

Surviving drafts show that composer and librettist worked closely together, with much revision and care. Bellini did not, as legend has it, make Romani rewrite 'Casta diva' ten times, but he did exact several drafts; he cut superfluous lines and used others to build unconventional musical structures the librettist had not foreseen.

Who chose to turn a violent melodrama into a classical tragedy in music? Alexandre Soumet's play was as much a Paris novelty in 1831 as Hernani had been the year before: it was less than four months old. The priestess whose love for an officer means sacrilege and treason was a theme fashionable in the early nineteenth century, combining as it did a neo-classical frame with a romantic shiver; in some versions, she has children by her lover. Soumet drew on Chateaubriand's Les Martyrs, a solemn harbinger of romanticism that placed the story, again fashionably, in Roman Gaul, but also on the Medea of Euripides. This pointed him to a sensational curtain: Norma kills her children and leaps off a high rock. Bellini and Romani, however, did away with both murder and suicide. The scene of renunciation and reconciliation they devised instead worked back into the opera as a whole. Not only did it give the heroine a new humanity and dignity; placing an outburst of collective emotion at the end meant breaking with the standard model in which such a finale closed the first half and, most often, a display of solo fireworks from the prima donna ended the opera.

According to a letter known to us only in Florimo's edition, Romani it was who insisted on ending the first half in unorthodox fashion with a highly dramatic trio. This would credit him with the new structure and temper of the work as a whole. Now that we have seen how Florimo faked parts of Bellini's letters to build up Romani's share in their joint work, this letter too must be thought unreliable; its style rings false as well. Until fresh evidence comes up, we should take Bellini to have had at least an equal part in shaping *Norma* away from sensationalism and towards high tragedy. He rightly thought the last scenes 'the best things I have done so far' (31 December 1831). The composer of one of the grandest half hours in all opera may be presumed to have had much to do with working out the fundamental dramatic conception.

Though *Norma* in our century has been regarded with some awe as a special work, to be performed when a dramatic soprano of outstanding gifts will take it on, in 1831 it took its chance as one more new opera, rehearsed in the standard three weeks. True, Pasta realized what was at stake: two or three days into rehearsals she declared that if she failed in the part she would give up the stage. She was right to be nervous. The first night came close to failure. We have to discard, as almost certainly a complete fake, the 'fiasco!!! fiasco!!! utter fiasco!!!' letter published by Florimo. Not only is it out of style; it contradicts what Bellini wrote in authentic letters.

There he reported that Act 1 fell flat, chiefly because the singers were tired out. They had rehearsed Act 2 that very morning: by the trio that brought down the curtain 'they could not sing a note' – so putting off twice over those who found such a curtain unorthodox. Act 2, however, went well and brought four curtain calls; the singers, we may presume, had recovered during the ballet that filled the interval. On the second and third nights the whole opera was a great success.

Tiredness is probably the basic explanation; the rushed timetable of Italian opera gave an uncertain start to more than one work later regarded as a staple. Bellini, however, added that a 'powerful person' (Duke Carlo Visconti di Modrone) had influenced the critics out of hostility to Pasta, while Pacini's mistress Countess Samoyloff had bribed a faction to hiss. This may be true. Visconti was a member of the supervisory board of La Scala, where Pasta, a Milanese singer, had conspicuously not been engaged till then; bribed or not, there were rival pro-Bellini and pro-Pacini factions. At all events the opera won through. Audiences, unusually hushed, came to thirty-four *Normas* in the first season alone.

In the next few years *Norma* was heard all over Europe; by 1838 a minor Naples theatre was performing it twice nightly. These repertory performances, some feeble to the verge of parody, went on until about 1880 (in Italy until about 1920). Bellini had at first been chary of letting any prima donna sing it other than Pasta or her rival Maria Malibran. The definitive performance, he thought, came at the August fair season of 1832. Pasta, by then fully sung in, 'drew many tears' from him; with a new, fierier tenor and mezzo, '*Norma* stunned the whole of Bergamo' (23 August 1832). Bellini could not forestall the later travesties, but, like us, he regarded the work as special.

What makes *Norma* special is its attainment of tragic grandeur through musical organization. Its kinship with Greek tragedy was clear to the young Wagner and, a little later, to the philosopher Schopenhauer: 'Seldom', he wrote, 'has the true tragic working out of the catastrophe, bringing with it the resignation and spiritual elevation of the [hero and heroine], stood out so purely motivated and so clearly expressed.'

The means was, on the one hand, melody, both 'the simple, noble, beautiful song' (Wagner) and 'the truth and power of declamation' (Verdi); on the other hand, the bending of the usual structures of Italian opera to create music drama.

Witness the climactic scenes Bellini thought his 'best things so far'. These begin as the faithless Roman proconsul Pollione is dragged on – caught in the act of violating the sanctuary; the news

pable jusque dans les bras de son amante! — En disant ces mots, elle s'a-
vance vers le lit de ses fils et lève le poignard... mais, saisie d'horreur à ce

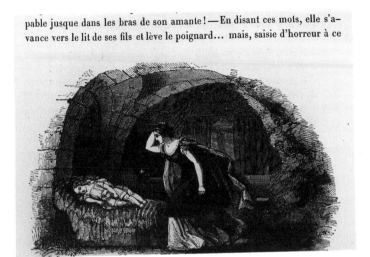

12 Norma threatens to kill her children: from a contemporary French publication
summarizing opera plots.

that he is trying to carry off her sometime rival Adalgisa has just led
Norma to strike the sacred gong and unleash patriotic war. The
opera till then has shown a powerful yet vulnerable woman: able in
her opening words to subdue the restive tribes (and her own father)
by force of personality, noble of diction in her prayer to the moon,
alternately fierce to her ex-lover and kind to the young novice he has
suborned, tempted to kill her children (it will prevent their falling
'slaves to a stepmother' in Rome) yet overwhelmed by her love for
them. What follows, from Pollione's entrance, is labelled in the
vocal score 'Scene and duet' and 'Scene and final aria'; Bellini called
them a duet and 'a finale made up of a concerted piece and a stretta'.
We might call them music drama attained by shaping and fusing the
elements of Italian operatic forms to make a continuous whole.

Norma as priestess should kill Pollione; she finds she cannot and
sends everyone else away on the pretext that she must interrogate
him. These exchanges, like others that follow later, bring back the
syllabic declamation of *La straniera*, yet their line – jagged, as befits

extreme states of feeling – seems inevitable where that seemed at times arbitrary: Bellini has fully absorbed his radical experiments into his mature style. When, in the next scene, Norma realizes the injustice she is about to commit by denouncing Adalgisa, and denounces herself instead, the lines 'Son io' ('It is I', a rising and falling fifth with a minim at the apex) and 'Norma non mente' ('Norma does not lie', a repeated E flat ending in an octave drop) could hardly be plainer, but it is the plainness of the heroic.

Before that comes 'In mia man alfin tu sei', neither a formal aria nor a duet as those were understood but a confrontation solemn in its unfolding, its syllabic word-setting varied only by the occasional acciaccatura or turn; as Norma offers Pollione his life if he will give up Adalgisa one or other 'speaks' in a segment of the melodic line. David Kimbell puts it well:

> The stillness, the tension, the stalemate of wills mirrored in the motionless calm of no fewer than twenty-six bars without a hint of modulation; the sudden vision of freedom, of escape, as the music opens up to the dominant C major; the inexorable return to the tonic and the opening theme as Pollione declines the bargain; the turn to D minor and the gradual acceleration in the delivery of the words as Norma begins to realize that she must despair of conquering Pollione's will – all these things represent a perfect fusion of music and meaning.

Norma's fury then explodes in a shower of arpeggios and turns and a rising sequence of trills: the Romans will perish, Adalgisa will go to the stake. This leads straight into the hard-driving cabaletta ('Già mi pasco ne' tuoi sguardi'), a continuing clash of wills now turned desperate, and to the resolution as Norma summons back the Gauls.

When she has denounced herself a terrified hush falls. How shall we describe what happens next? 'Qual cor tradisti' looks like the slow section of a concertato finale, with first the soprano, then the tenor, finally the bass and the chorus joining in. But (Bellini's labels notwithstanding) it will not lead to a conventional stretto, nor is it a conventional largo.

13 Alessandro Sanquirico's backcloth for the forest scene in the original
production of *Norma*, 1831.

A soaring five-note melodic kernel over a rocking accompaniment, repeated at different points in the scale to an unchanging
rhythm: here is simplicity itself, varied only by semiquaver or triplet
decorations at the ends of phrases, and by a modulation that gives a
sense of opening out. Yet this is the music at once of stasis and of reconciliation, with death, voluntarily chosen, to both Norma and Pollione the only possible token of love. So it will be, nearly sixty years
later, to another pair who have blocked for each other all the roads
they could take, the lovers in Ibsen's *Rosmersholm*. Rebecca and Ros-
mer attain 'the higher love', but the cost of their 'ennobling' is
renunciation and death. Slow though the English-speaking public is
to use such language, 'ennobling' – as Schopenhauer perceived – is
what goes on in 'Qual cor tradisti': Norma and Pollione find in their
consciences the strength to purge themselves of sin – of anger, pride,

and lust; love springs back, but it leads to the funeral pyre. When Oroveso and the chorus join in, their words (most likely unheard) express a hope that all this may yet be untrue, but their music saturates the climax in the overcoming of loss to attain serenity.

In most of what follows, the community and the doomed lovers are again musically at one though their words oppose them. To begin with we do hear the Gauls question Norma in urgent exchanges. She remembers the children, first as 'mine', then, significantly – turning to Pollione – as 'ours'. Over a calmly steady stepwise accompaniment, she confesses to her father in a plangent arioso and begs him to look after them; the chorus joins Oroveso in expressing horror. She then, amid general silence, rises twice to high G (fermata) and, the second time, to high A and B followed by a long, chromatic, wandering descent: the entire creature stretched out in her plea for mercy.

Another silence launches, over a repeated sighing figure, her cantabile 'Deh! non volerli vittime', a heroine's lament, heart-rending yet contained. Oroveso resists, then gives way: 'love has won', reconciliation is complete. The chorus have joined in as the first, E minor, section gives way to E major; but although their words move from hostility to curse, Bellini keeps them as a musical ground to the principals' anguished exchanges. The libretto shows them baying Norma and Pollione to the stake; the music, until the few headlong final bars, has the sorrowing collectivity bear up the principals in their greatness and woe.

From its quiet start – middle B repeated six times, three of them dotted notes, with an elegiac flick at the end – this cantabile rises slowly through a series of four two-bar phrases all beginning with the tonic. Such insistence – Lippmann has shown – at once brings 'enormous expressive intensification' and delays the climax, another plea that soars twice to G, the second time to high B, each time descending stepwise in triplets: the plea of the sorrowing universe. This triggers the major section. The drama moves, the woodwinds launch a new motif, a hungry phrase answered by a calming one, the first taken up by Norma, the other by Oroveso; the father relents; the orchestra further enriches the texture with a short phrase repeated, climbing semitone by semitone amid deliberate dissonance and much holding back – forerunner of Wagner's chromatic sequences in *Tristan und Isolde* – the tension enhanced by a slow crescendo that leads up to fortissimo and quickly abates; the whole process is repeated; the key reverts to E minor (allegro agitato assai) and the scene hurtles to its end amid anguished farewells.

'No one', Alfred Einstein wrote in 1935, 'knows what music is who does not come away from *Norma* filled to overflowing with the last pages of this act.' Not only do they show the overcoming of the baser self by the three principals and even – regardless of the words – by the community at large. Bellini has fused several textual episodes in different metres to create what Kimbell terms 'one single musical form, drawing out the tears and pathos and despair of the catastrophe into one long, sustained ecstatic cantabile'. This saturation of the form in ecstatic sound is a mark of romanticism in music. Yet if we ask where Bellini could have found a model for this finale the answer must be in Rossini – in *Semiramide* (the ensemble 'Quel mesto gemito', its hushed ostinato a forerunner of 'Qual cor tradisti'), above all in the finale of *Guillaume Tell*: there the saturation of collective feeling in music denotes universal solemn joy, but the means are not unlike those Bellini uses for an act of collective mourning at the fall of a heroine. Both composers hold the romantic depth of emotion within a form whose dignity remains classical.[15]

Grandeur allied to innovative form marks the rest of Norma's part. An old-fashioned reviewer of the first London performance complained that the work 'has no arias'. He meant that only Pollione has a double aria, its halves uninterrupted by anyone else. Her declamation apart, Norma sings always with other soloists or the chorus lending her at least a musical frame. This enhances her stature: her very first scene, lasting over a quarter of an hour, compasses a march, an eloquent declamatory recitative, a double aria which flute and orchestra anticipate and the chorus either joins in or interrupts.

We see and hear in her the priestess able to guide her people, but also the troubled, loving woman isolated from them.

A pendant to the Act 2 finale, this scene too rises in 'Casta diva' to an ecstatic climax achieved in part by the same means of slow crescendo, sequences rising and delayed, and gradual intensification of orchestral sound, in part by brief oscillations in and out of the minor – the key of F, in Failla's words, 'touched, left, and taken up again as if it burned'. The melody of 'Casta diva' has always been famous even when Bellini's reputation was in a trough. It unfolds in leisurely $\frac{12}{8}$ (andante sostenuto assai) through fifteen bars without a repetition, and at the fortissimo climax, delayed until bars 13 and 14, the voice expands to high B flat and begins a slow looping descent, a bright bird circling down the moonlit sky.

Placing the climax near the end of a melody was an aid to romantic intensity which Bellini pioneered. It occurs in several other numbers, most notably in the two duets for Norma and Adalgisa and the dynamic trio at the end of Act 1. The first duet, 'Sola, furtiva al tempio', with delicate exactness fixes the situation: as Adalgisa confesses, Norma's realization that their stories are alike prompts her to speak, as yet only to herself. Her recitative self-communings ride over the anticipation in flute and orchestra of the main theme, showing this exquisite melody to be 'as much the music of [her] heart as it is of Adalgisa's' (Kimbell), and in the remainder of the duet the voices interact until the growing sympathy between the women brings them together in melismatic thirds. This effect, similarly justified, closes the Act 2 duet as well, a three-part structure whose andante middle section, 'Mira o Norma', is a further stroke of Bellinian simplicity, the voice delivering, chiefly in steps of a tone or semitone, its burden of grace.

Norma's full dramatic stature emerges in the trio and, after the interval, in the scene where she thinks of killing her children ('Dormono entrambi'). The trio is nothing if not strenuous – an organized tempest; how could Bellini ever have been thought a mere 'elegiac' composer? Norma opens it – she has just realized who Adalgisa's suitor is – with a burst of tremendous minatory *fioriture* and descending scales ('Oh non tremare'); twice she rises to high C. She goes on to rally Adalgisa to her side in an urgent $\frac{9}{8}$ (andante marcato, 'Oh! di qual sei tu vittima'). We hear Adalgisa change camps musically: though the words show her alienated from Pollione, she sings at first with him and then, as the melody softens and expands ('Fonte d'eterne lagrime'), joins Norma; in declamatory exchanges she refuses to follow the 'destiny' her lover presses on her. Norma it is who again launches the final driving allegro – all three eventually sing together, borne along on rhythm and anger; Norma's five high Bs top a stretto that keeps her above the stave throughout.

If the trio belies the 'elegiac' composer, the prelude to Act 2 belies the 'inadequate' writer for orchestra. A sighing string figure, tear-laden, gives way to the saddest of Bellini's 'long, long, long' melodies, an unwinding of lonely grief over the pulsating, repeated *pp* quavers that are his sign for inner pain. Verdi would be no more expressive or concise in the prelude to the last act of *La traviata*, a piece inspired by this one. When Norma appears, dagger in hand, fragments of the first part of the prelude intersperse her efforts to steel herself. A little ostinato figure holds her back; as she dissolves in maternal feeling ('Teneri figli') she takes up the melody of lonely grief and follows it through to the end. Yet she talks herself into one more attempt; raises the dagger; melts again, now to a quick series of alternating chords. In one way this is a declamatory scene for a powerful singing actress; in another it is a miniature double aria, fined down to essentials almost as Verdi's were to be sixty years later in *Falstaff*. Bellini here conjures the forms of Italian opera into music drama.

Norma is the real matter of *Norma*. When she is on stage the opera is vibrantly alive. The rest works on another plane. It has often been called uneven. Some things work only if the singer can put across Italian words and if the audience can understand them; if neither condition is met, even Norma's declamatory scenes can fall flat. This tells us only that Bellini's choice medium was the union of word and music.

Bellini himself wrote of Pollione's aria, the cabaletta especially, and his duet with Adalgisa that the Milan audience did not like them – 'and neither do I'. Another letter, though, makes clear that he did not like them as the 'cold' Milan singers performed them. At Bergamo eight months later, everything was 'more alive, and spirited'; the new tenor Domenico Reina sang the cabaletta 'with such fire . . . that everyone thought I had written a new one' (28, 31 December 1831, 23 August 1832). Bellini was right in that spirited performers can make a good deal of these numbers, and so can an impressive bass in Oroveso's two arias with chorus; but their music, though well cut, remains somewhat generic. Even the cabaletta to 'Casta diva' ('Ah! bello a me ritorna', a tune recycled from two previous operas) is not much more than highly efficient in its context.

The military music is the real stumbling-block. Not the headlong chorus 'Guerra! guerra!'. Old Zingarelli, when he first read it in score, exclaimed that it was 'just right' and 'fine' – 'and how very barbaric!' So it is. The score he was looking at may not have included the visionary coda, in which the warriors who have been baying for blood suddenly fall to prayer in a halo of harp arpeggios and trills; Bellini cut it after the first performance for the sake of speed – this chorus had already given him much trouble – but the uncanny effect was in print and opera houses now generally perform it. (Norma, like many Italian operas of its day, has no one final text authorized by the composer; this is the most notable of several variants.)

What does strike non-Italian ears as incongruous, even comic, is the march that precedes and ends 'Casta diva'. The druids, it suggests, run a particularly tinny village band, yet it frames a scene of mystery and prophecy. This comes of the vogue for military band music launched by the French Revolution. The fashion lingered on in Italy, part of an innocent delight in such things as the Bersaglieri tootling at the double, bugles to their lips, cock plumes bobbing on their helmets – a spectacle that now raises smiles from a hardened BBC TV newscaster like Michael Buerk, yet in their home country these light infantrymen are thought a crack regiment. Norma's hangover from revolutionary band music acts like an air pocket.

'Guerra! guerra!', together with Oroveso's prophecy that divine intervention will 'free Gaul from the enemy's eagles', have persuaded many people that *Norma* is an Italian nationalist opera preaching revolt against Austria. In the first fifteen years or so of its career it was nothing of the kind. It could be given at Cremona in 1838 before the visiting Austrian Emperor without a hitch; the singers lined up to perform the imperial anthem to general cheers. Only in the immediate run-up to the 1848 revolutions did the words quoted trigger nationalist demonstrations, and again in the run-up to the 1859 war of independence. In less fevered times the theme of a revolt directed against Rome held problems for Italian nationalists. Mazzini, who thought his contemporary Bellini an un-'progressive' artist, launched a cult of Rome as both the necessary capital of a united Italy and a beacon to the world. Later on Mussolini blatantly exploited imperial Rome and its symbols. The film *Anni difficili* (1948), a satire on the Fascist period, shows party officials at a performance of *Norma* alarmed to hear outcries against the capital of the Fascist empire.[16]

Bellini's relation to Italy would soon become a problem in another sense. What it meant to him is examined in chapter 6. Meanwhile he had created in *Norma* one of the few works we may confidently place in a category much talked about when he was growing up – the sublime.

5   False steps

With *Norma* the thirty-year-old composer was aware of having created something special. Eight days after the first performance the Milan newspaper, though still carping, had to admit the work's success with the audience; a poem in Milanese dialect, published soon after, named the composer as second only to Rossini. An opera at first controverted – 'persecuted' was Bellini's term – would clearly do well.

Bellini, however, was finding out over pirated performances of *Sonnambula* how difficult it was to translate success into a continued flow of income. His plan, announced in July 1830, to retire in four years had been optimistic. A slow worker with high ambitions needed to raise his game beyond the Italian opera composer's routine. Bellini had done so twice, first with *Pirata* and *Straniera*, then, after the mishap over *Zaira*, with *Sonnambula* and *Norma*; each time he had found a new style that delighted the Italian public. The next step, an obvious one, was to work in a rich capital city – London or Paris; that too would mean moving on as an artist. Bellini took it, but not till May 1833. Meanwhile the delay involved him in several false steps, not wholly of his own making.

Paris especially had been a magnet to Italian composers since the mid eighteenth century. In Bellini's lifetime the shining example was Rossini, who had made a new career by helping to invent French grand opera; he had also earned a great deal of money in London. Bellini was well aware of the possibilities. As early as November

1828, after the success of *Pirata*, he had come close to agreeing with
the manager of the King's Theatre – the London opera house – to put
on that work and write a new one; but he was also aware of how
expensive London was for visitors (it was the equivalent of Tokyo
today) and broke off negotiations when the fee offered remained
3,000 francs below what he wanted. 'To go for next to nothing would
not have been good for my self-esteem', he told Florimo; when the
time came he might after all do better in Paris (22 November 1828).

If he did not try for Paris or London in early 1832 the reason was
presumably that Giuditta Turina could not have gone with him.
Thanks to Florimo's bonfire of letters we know nothing of their relations in the previous two years. That they were still good appears
from what came next. Bellini went back to Sicily for the first time
since 1824 or 1825; also for the first time, Turina went with him – not
to Sicily (unthinkable that he should introduce his mistress to his
family) but to Naples, where he spent six weeks on the way out, and a
few days on the way back.

This was carrying a bit further the policy of discreet 'friendship'
and of the blind eye turned on it by the Turina and Cantù families.
Turina travelled with her brother and found separate lodgings; as they
all went off in early January she could be said to be wintering in a mild
climate. That southern winter turned out often blustery and wet and
disrupted Bellini's plans: steamboats, then in their infancy, could not
ply between Naples and Sicily on the expected dates, bad roads within
Sicily grew dangerous as torrents – unbridged – came in spate.

On their arrival in Naples Turina at last met Francesco Florimo.
They became friends; the friendship was to survive the break-up of
the affair with Bellini and, by many years, his death. She was soon
taken ill with 'pains', probably her usual cramps, that went on for
three weeks. According to what Bellini wrote after the breach, she
caused him 'anguish' at one point by flirting with an 'old man', but it
is hard to know what to make of this and other retrospective charges;
the 'flirtation' may have amounted to little. She stayed on in Naples
for the two months that Bellini and Florimo were away in Sicily (25

February to 25 April). The lovers (and the brother) then made a leisurely journey back up the peninsula, stopping in Rome and Florence and reaching Milan about the beginning of June.

In Naples, and still more in Sicily, Bellini was hailed as a returning hero. His latest and finest works had not yet arrived, but performances of *Capuleti* in Naples and Palermo, and of *Pirata* at Messina, roused enthusiasm; Catania made up for being able to put on no more than concert extracts by throwing in performances of what sound like a dire tragedy and yet worse poems and eulogies by fifteen local authors. Bellini attended them all, took many curtain calls, was crowned with bay leaves or roses, and made gracious acknowledgments. In Naples he met the Queen Mother and was named a royal academician, at Catania the municipality put on a triumphal entry and an official concert, Palermo offered a banquet and a concert by upper-class amateurs at which the Genius of Sicily inscribed a bust of the composer. Tunes from *Pirata*, *Straniera*, and *Capuleti* resounded. It was a consecration.

In more private moments Bellini found his old room again at the Naples Conservatorio, where he stayed, and his old teacher Zingarelli, to whom he dedicated the score of *Norma*. The students made much of him; between the lines of Florimo's conventional account (with Bellini modestly claiming no more than luck) we may guess at a southern occasion, the students genuinely warm, their ambition whetted by the sight of the local graduate made good, the still young great man dispensing benevolence. At Catania the reunion with his family was at the heart of his month's stay, but it has left almost no trace other than his thank-you letter asking to be remembered to many cousins and aunts. We may guess at uproar, delight, feasts.

At Palermo Bellini made friends with a group of contemporaries centred on the lawyer Filippo Santocanale, to whom from then on he was to write frankly about his professional though not his personal life. These youngish men he described as 'the old guard' or 'the tanners', a Palermo slang term which according to the biographer Francesco Pastura implied dealings with easy women. Bellini's letters show that some of the 'tanners' were – as later English slang would put it – stage-door johnnies, but what if anything this tells us of his own conduct during his Palermo stay (of not quite three weeks) is guesswork. A pleasing story that rings true has him visiting incognito with some of these friends a church where the organist was a Bellinomane, and pretending to run down his own music; when the organist had spluttered his indignation to a finish and stalked off, Bellini took over and played 'Casta diva': stupefaction! disclosure! enthusiasm all round!

This double homecoming to Naples and Sicily must have meant a good deal to Bellini. Not that it made him lose his business head. In Naples he discussed a proposal to write an opera for the San Carlo, but turned it down because he could not be sure of getting the right singers: this with him was a fixed point. He was free to enter into a contract wherever he wished; in May he did so for the 1833 carnival-Lent season at La Fenice, Venice, where the same impresario who had mounted *Capuleti* there – Alessandro Lanari – would be in charge and the prima donna would be Giuditta Pasta.[17]

This was a false step for a number of reasons, most of them unforeseeable. La Fenice was a theatre with high prestige, owned by an association of upper-class people and run by an exacting committee, but takings were relatively low and it was touch and go whether the impresario could break even. Lanari, as it happened, had trouble with both the women singers he had undertaken to provide. Giulia Grisi, who had created Adalgisa in *Norma*, was under long-term contract to him, but she broke it and fled to Paris, where she launched a new, splendid career; the La Fenice committee exacted compensation from Lanari for the loss of her services. Giuditta Pasta's fee of 1,000 francs per performance meant higher costs; the theatre owners reluctantly agreed that Lanari should meet them by raising the price of admission, but Pasta feared that touchy Venice opera-goers would blame her: she insisted on a clause barring any price increase. Everyone had a cue for discontent or apprehension. Even without a price increase part of the audience, which in a gossipy Italian city

knew this background, were set against the expensive and by then
not always well-tuned Pasta; they might exploit the first sign of trouble.[18]

Bellini may have made an avoidable mistake when, for the third
time running, he laid the chances of success on a collaboration with
Pasta. The old saw 'third time unlucky' has some basis: after two hits
a touch of carelessness may set in. Yet he had every excuse: Pasta had
just triumphed as Norma; she was to open the Venice carnival season
in the part before creating his new work; she was his friend and
might become his mother-in-law. She further enhanced her stature
when, at the Bergamo August fair – soon after his return from Naples
– she and Norma triumphed more convincingly than ever: the whole
work had come together, and her performance made Bellini weep.[19]
All this helps to explain why he let her persuade him into a late and
ill-advised choice of subject for his new opera.

Yet another hazard – Bellini was probably not at once aware of it –
was that in the autumn and winter of 1832–3 Romani had taken on
more work than at any other point in his career: five librettos, for
operas to be performed in three cities, with still more pressing on
behind. In strong contrast with his punctuality over Norma a year earlier, Romani let July and early August go by without agreeing a subject; then Bellini was in Bergamo and, briefly, at the Turinas' house at
Casalbuttano until about 20 September; only sometime between 24
September and 6 October did Romani settle – probably with Bellini's
agreement – on Queen Christina of Sweden, a subject drawn from a
ramshackle trilogy by Alexandre Dumas père. By 3 November,
though, Bellini had persuaded Romani – 'with difficulty' – to change
to a new subject, Beatrice di Tenda.

What had happened? We now have the first four scenes of Cristina
di Svezia in Romani's draft, as much as he had managed to write in the
intervening month. They are not promising; they read like the start
of a generic, conventional work. If Bellini saw them, as is likely, he
may well have had misgivings. But he was also influenced by Pasta.

She had seen a narrative ballet about Beatrice di Tenda and had told him of her enthusiasm: she saw herself as the long-suffering heroine, who at the end goes to the scaffold with all the dignity of Mary Queen of Scots in Schiller's play. Not for the first or last time, a leading lady went for a meaty part without worrying too much about the viability of the work as a whole. Bellini acquiesced and, to begin with, was fully persuaded. Romani feared too close a likeness to *Anna Bolena* and was angry at the waste of *Cristina* (he was to recycle it – twenty-two years later). It was not a good decision.

A row of dates signposts the path to failure. Bellini's new opera was scheduled as the last of the Venice season. This normally meant that it would open sometime in February, at the latest very early in March; the actual date set was 20 February. Once the new subject had been agreed on 3 November, the usual forty-day period for finishing the libretto would have allowed Bellini about seven weeks to compose the music, as much as he had had for *Sonnambula*; he would have had a little longer still if, as was normal practice, Romani delivered some of the words within a week or two.

On 8 December Bellini and Pasta arrived in Venice to start rehearsals of *Norma*. Whether Romani had supplied any words for *Beatrice* is unclear; perhaps not, for Bellini wrote 'I am in good health and if my poet gave me material to work on my mind too would be at rest' (10 December). By 12 January his health was beginning to suffer as well: the cause was overwork and the fault was Romani's – 'the god of idleness!' – who so far had given him only two numbers in Act 1.

Meanwhile, however, the impresario Lanari had enlisted (on 14 December) the help of the police. Back in Milan, he summoned Romani; though he protested (23 December), blaming the late choice of subject and his other commitments, he was unable to find a convincing excuse as he had over *Straniera*: the police made him go to Venice, where he arrived about 23 January, presumably in a foul temper. By 27 January Bellini hoped 'tomorrow to start on the finale of Act 1, if Romani gives it me'. It must have been doubtful by then whether *Beatrice* could open on 20 February, though a 'friend' later claimed that Bellini could have met the deadline.

Relations between composer and librettist had soured: in a note to Romani of about this date Bellini used the formal 'voi'; until then they had used the intimate 'tu'. He wrote that he had been working 'like a dog' and had already once failed to find Romani at his lodgings; he therefore asked sarcastically to be warned 'if matters more important than the libretto call you away from home'. Yet on 14 February Bellini was still having to turn out and pester Romani for more words. Romani, for his part, had been infuriated by the police summons; as well as with Bellini he had to cope with Donizetti who, from Florence, was crying out for the libretto of *his* new opera – it was even later than *Beatrice*'s. The last stages of composition are undocumented but were certainly rushed. When the opera opened – late – an important duet for the women had been left unfinished; it was scrapped. For the heroine's crucial last number Bellini resorted to digging out a piece from *Bianca e Fernando*, not fully adequate.[20]

A further worry was the La Fenice company. It was, Bellini wrote, 'ghastly'; only Pasta, 'a safe anchor in any shipwreck', had carried *Norma* through on the opening night of the season (12, 27 January 1833). The tenor was famous but old, the mezzo mediocre, and the bass useless, so much so that he had to be replaced; the new bass was good, but he could come – at Bellini's entreaty – only late in the season; when he did arrive, three numbers had to be adapted to suit his voice. The upshot was that the first night of *Beatrice*, already reset for 6 March, had to be put off once again, to 16 March. Bellini had always insisted on a good company of singers before he agreed to write an opera. Why not this time? He wagered all on Pasta, and presumably chose to ignore the mediocre singers the impresario had taken on to offset his expensive star.

The cost of depending on Pasta soon became clear. The repeated delay irked those in Venice who were already prejudiced against her. Two days before the first night, the editor of the local newspaper – who till then had dealt with each production even-handedly – published a complaint from a fictitious subscriber: was it fair to the audience to give the new opera only in the last week of the season? He made fun of Bellini for taking a whole year to write an opera, and added for good measure that this one was really destined for London – Venice was a mere launching-pad. That would have been enough to annoy the Venetians – according to Bellini, 'the most gossipy and petty-minded audience in the world' – if it had not probably mirrored an existing ill temper (July 1834). Romani for his part prefaced the libretto with one of his lofty apologias, in which he called the opera a 'fragment': 'unavoidable circumstances' had 'changed its structure, colours, and characteristics'; it needed 'every indulgence'. Almost an invitation to hiss.

And hiss they did – part of the audience, at any rate – even before the curtain went up. They also called out 'Norma!' whenever they thought a passage sounded like the earlier opera: at a time when composers wrote one new work after another and inevitably used a common language, hostile opera-goers liked to spot 'reminiscences'. 'I thought I was at a fair', Bellini wrote nine days later, 'so much so that Sicilian haughtiness took full possession of me': when applause came, as it did after a few numbers, he refused to take a bow. The remaining five performances drew a large audience, somewhat better inclined. All the same, *Beatrice* was a flop.

Bellini did not despair. These things happened. *Zaira*, he recalled, had got its own back in *Capuleti*, *Norma* had triumphed over its initial difficulties: *Beatrice*, 'which I consider not unworthy of her sisters', might yet succeed elsewhere (25 March 1833). Later that year he proposed to 'renew' the cabalettas of the last two arias, including the crucial one he had had to draft in from *Bianca*; this might mean adapting, but more likely replacing them.[21] In the conditions of Italian opera he would need to be on hand or at least to know the singers; the opportunity did not come up. *Beatrice*, unrevised, did catch on and had a fair Italian career down to the 1870s. Revivals in our own century have been tentative.

The reason is all too clear; it soon became clear to Bellini. The subject, he wrote, was 'horrible' (11 April 1834). As Romani was to

acknowledge, it was 'too melancholy and surpassingly monotonous'. Beatrice's marriage to the tyrant she has helped to power is in
ruins from the start; he is determined to get rid of her, and he sends
her to the block after having been offered a pretext to put her and her
alleged lover to torture – twice. Beatrice is steadily noble, her Henry
VIII-like husband steadily brutal but for one unconvincing lapse
(and his baritone arias are no less mellifluous for what Bellini called
his 'disgusting' character). Dramatic change comes only from the
mezzo and the tenor, both subsidiary. All this is reflected in the
music. Much in the score is beautiful and well crafted, but it fails to
add up: *Beatrice* is less effective than the uneven, at times juvenile
Pirata.

Why did Pasta and Bellini think so well of it as a subject? She in
particular may have joined in a cult of unrelieved pathos that
belonged to the eighteenth century more than to full-blown romanticism. It was the stock in trade of sentimental drama and of gothic
novels with their endlessly persecuted heroines; it still informed
Shelley's *The Cenci*, written a few years before the Italian play of 1825
that was the source of both the *Beatrice* ballet and the opera; it shaped
some of Pasta's most successful roles – Paisiello's Nina and Rossini's Desdemona. The Romantic age – Bellini was normally aware –
looked for greater variety and surprise.

That his music does not convey the horror of torture as Puccini's
was to do in *Tosca* and *Turandot* perhaps stands to Bellini's credit. The
chorus in which the women three times anxiously question and the
men three times describe the stages of Orombello's torture, all in
unchanging melodic patterns, is meant to convey relentlessness;
each time, though, the men's answering strophe is a regulation
swinging, bouncing tune, not bad in itself but incongruous. Elsewhere the chorus has a good deal to do. It is more effective when
framing the principals – as it often does, sometimes in innovatory
ways – than in its own numbers. Some of these anticipate Verdi's
choruses in *Trovatore*, but sound both forcible and feeble.

Nowhere, in fact, does Bellini appear as completely the 'elegiac' composer of myth as in *Beatrice*. Pathos rules, only in part because the subject allows few openings for anything else. The best numbers are all slow and melancholy. Soaring, arc-shaped melodies distinguish the heroine's music, in particular her arioso 'Deh! se mi amasti un giorno' (with interesting low woodwind accompaniment), and the cantabile sections of both her opening and her final aria. As Lippmann has shown, Bellini stretches out the melodic arc to draw from it the utmost expressiveness, yet lightens it with coloratura to avoid over-intensity; this gives a sense of Beatrice rising above her horrible plight.

The finest things in the work are all concerted pieces dominated by Beatrice, though the tenor (from his offstage cell) launches the trio before the execution, the simply beautiful 'Angiol di pace', adapted from *Zaira*. Of the two quintets, the first ('Ah! tal onta io meritai') is the slow section of the Act 1 finale, the second ('Al tuo fallo ammenda festi') brings the trial scene in Act 2 to a climax as Orombello retracts his confession and exonerates Beatrice. Both do indeed recall *Norma* – the first by saturating the hearer in sound as Beatrice's voice floats above the waves, the second in the grandeur of its outline.

Notwithstanding its musical splendours *Beatrice* lacks propulsion. Again and again it falls into the perfunctory, one or two mechanical crescendos included – clearly the outcome of the anxious rush amid which Bellini had to work. Elsewhere what ails it is the basic flaw of the subject, nowhere more plainly than in Filippo's soliloquy ('Rimorso in lei?'). In this recitative he hears Beatrice offstage being led from the torture chamber back to her cell, wonders whether he should not after all reprieve her, then changes his mind on getting news of a popular revolt in her favour. This was obviously meant to reverse the effect of Norma's soliloquy as she wonders whether to kill her children – a 'reminiscence' less happy than the two quintets just mentioned: though the orchestra well expresses Beatrice's quiet suffering, Filippo's vocal line does not convince. Norma's inner struggle flowed from her whole being, musical as well as dramatic. Filippo is a stage villain for whose crisis of conscience nothing has prepared us; his self-questioning sounds like bluster.

It is a great pity. The more successful *Norma*-like passages show that Bellini could still work at that high level while moving yet further away from the conventional scheme of the solo aria. From an ambitious composer, though, they suggest a moment of treading water. In one way and another Bellini depended too much on Pasta's known strengths as well as on her judgment – and his motives may have been personal (the hope of marrying Clelia) as well as professional.

The Venice season brought more false steps. The first meant a breach with Romani. On 6 January, when he was still waiting for Romani to come to Venice (under protest) and yield up some words, Bellini wrote, 'I think this will be the last libretto he will write for me: he will con me no more . . .'[22] That might have been a passing mood, but when Romani did come tension remained high. Bellini was irked to find that local opinion blamed the delay on him, all the more when the Venice newspaper confirmed this prejudice; Romani's foreword to the libretto, calling the opera a 'fragment', made matters worse. After his experiences on the first night Bellini got a 'friend' to write to the newspaper pointing out that the delay had been caused by the librettist (and prolonged by the change of bass). This would have been rash even if the 'friend', while keeping to a neutral tone, had not got one important fact wrong and had not stated another that was true but inopportune. Romani, he claimed, had written not one word of the proposed *Cristina* by late October, when Bellini asked for a change to *Beatrice*, but had merely brought it up then as a possible subject. He also disclosed that the police had forced Romani to come.

After eight collaborations Bellini should have known that Romani was not the man to take this lying down; perhaps he no longer cared. All the same, he can hardly have expected the venom of the librettist's reply. It took the form of two letters to the newspapers, one for Venice, the other for Milan. The Milan letter held the worst venom. It appeared a day before the other, which had to travel from Milan to Venice, so both were probably written at the same time; there is no question of Romani's having yielded (as one biographer has suggested) to an impulse that came over him once the controversy was under way. He meant to injure Bellini in the city where he lived and was best known.

In both letters he alleged that Bellini had reserved the right to choose the subject of the new opera, but had failed to do so all the way from July to November; the delay was therefore his fault, and Romani had agreed to discard *Cristina* and write *Beatrice* only as an act of self-sacrifice and out of 'affection for Bellini'. All this was untrue. Where Romani did score was in elaborately hinting that both the delay and the switch to *Beatrice* came of the influence exercised over the composer by his 'Minerva' – an obvious allusion to Pasta, caustic but no worse.

So far, the letter might have been thought to answer, more acrimoniously, one wrong statement with another, and all might have blown over. In the Milan version, however, Romani added that the delay came of Bellini's having vanished: he was 'dallying, a new Rinaldo, on Armida's island'. The enchantress Armida, as 'everyone' in Milanese society was bound to know, meant Turina. This was scandalous – all the more because (as we shall see, and as Romani probably knew) the affair with Turina was approaching a crisis.

The breach was complete. When the squib of the 'Armida' letter went off in early April, Bellini was back in Milan. More venomous exchanges went on in the newspapers, but he had no apparent share in them. About 10 or 12 April he, Pasta, and her husband left for London to take part in the opera season that ran from April to July.

The Italian opera business was a school of hard knocks. Under its pressures many called one another scoundrel and worse, and then ended – after an exchange of self-justifying arguments – by working together once more. Within less than a year Bellini was ready to contemplate working with Romani if a possible contract for Naples came off and if the two of them could be there at the same time: 'I should like', he told Florimo, 'to return good for ill to that wrong-headed but highly talented man' (11 March 1834). Then, just over a month later, an Italian theatrical agent proposed a reconciliation. This man got Romani, in a letter to a third person, to say that he had always loved Bellini and that the Venice trouble had been partly the work of the composer's 'misguided friends'. Bellini by then had found out the drawbacks of working with an inexperienced librettist. He jumped at the chance of getting Romani back for his next opera in Italy.

His letter to Romani made no excuses. The offence, he wrote, was not his: he had had to defend himself before the Venice public; in any case everyone knew that Romani took on too much work and was habitually late. He refuted the allegation that he had idled away the summer of 1832 – on the contrary, it was he who had been continually at Romani's door: 'doesn't your conscience reproach you for all the untruths you uttered? . . . And what needless insults besides did you not add to what you called your defence?' To Romani's profession of continuing love Bellini said it could not be true but countered with his own; this was a ritual element in theatre quarrels, and need not be taken literally. He ended: 'Let us draw a veil over so many misfortunes and, if possible, let us repair them with mutual repentance . . .' Romani, he insisted, should place an announcement to that effect in the chief Italian newspapers: the two of them could then resume without shame 'our attachment that was born with my career and I hope will cease with my life' (July 1834).[23]

Romani took his time: his satisfactory reply arrived some four months later. By then he had solved his problem by accepting the editorship of the Turin government newspaper: it paid him the salary of a high civil servant, more than twice what he had earned writing librettos, with a pension to come. No longer under pressure, he was willing to write a libretto now and then.

Bellini responded confidently. Romani should 'write for me only' and should demand twice his usual fee; provided that he wrote what he really wanted to and thought he could deliver, Bellini would be happy to work with him in one city or another: 'I will choose the one likeliest to bring fame and money' (7 October 1834). When he had a contract for two new operas for Naples he urged Romani 'with all the vehemence of my heart' to write the librettos; 'I always' – he admitted – 'give you trouble by being hard to please', but he insisted that the librettos must be ready in time; he wanted to know if Romani could 'in all conscience' promise that (4 January 1835).[24] Three months went by without an answer. The Naples contract had by then been cancelled; Bellini's death soon followed.

He had set a high value on Romani's work, but had dealt with him as one sovereign professional to another; after *Beatrice* he was no longer prepared to wait on Romani unconditionally. It was Florimo who made up fulsome compliments to the librettist and printed them as Bellini's. When Romani next undertook to write a libretto – for Mercadante at the Italian opera in Paris – it never came; the composer was driven frantic; the opera reached the stage months late, with a libretto by someone else.

One more reason why Bellini was tense during that Venice carnival and Lent was the presence of Giuditta Turina. It was the start of their falling out.

We have the usual problem that their accounts of the episode were all written after the breach, in self-justification whether conscious or not. Her 'flirting' at Naples a year earlier had made Bellini jealous – or so he recalled. How they got on during the rest of 1832 we do not know; that Bellini spent only part of the summer by the lake, and the rest alone in Milan, proves nothing. In August the two of them apparently met in Bergamo during the *Norma* performances, but Turina went with her husband.

Trouble, according to her version, started in the winter of 1832–3: Bellini in Venice heard from some busybody that back in Milan a man was courting her and had stayed till 2 a.m.; he insisted that she should join him in Venice. Ferdinando Turina, meanwhile, had received an anonymous letter denouncing the affair, presumably chose to disregard it, but was against her going. With difficulty she got her husband's leave and went; this she later thought a false step. In Venice Bellini 'treated [her] very badly', but by the time both were again in Milan and he went off to London they were 'on excellent terms'. The storm broke in May. Though she had begged him not to, Bellini wrote her some compromising letters; they fell into her husband's hands. Ferdinando at once threw her out and sued for a legal separation.[25]

Turina's account thus far seems plausible, though looking back she may have taken a rosy view of the 'excellent terms' she and Bellini had been on at the time of his departure. Someone, perhaps a member of the Turina family, may have put the compromising letters under Ferdinando's nose: he had apparently ignored all previous evidence, Romani's 'Armida' letter included, and needed to be jockeyed into a situation where he had to react. Giuditta later suggested that if she had thought the relationship with Bellini was over she could, even at that point, have managed a reconciliation with her husband. As it was, she went back to her family and started a long, difficult wrangle with the Turinas over money.

What happened next is unclear. On 26 August Bellini, by then in Paris, was planning a trip to Geneva so as to get news of Turina's dealings with her husband, about which he was still 'in the dark', and to 'find out whether my drawing closer to G. would be delicate or not'.[26] This points to a meeting at which they would decide whether to live together, or at any rate in the same city; but there is no evidence that Bellini went to Geneva.

According to Turina's later, somewhat jumbled account, Bellini to begin with asked her forgiveness about the letters and hoped that she would not give him up; she for her part was ready to join him or to meet him now and then, as he wished. In September, however, he wrote that over the previous eighteen months his love had cooled; his motive, she said, was 'the Venice jealousy, and other gossip people fed him in Paris'. Turina fell ill; she would not reply, but when her friends wrote on her behalf during the winter of 1833–4 'he answered them all by denigrating my reputation to excuse his conduct, and he took not the slightest responsibility for my situation'. His talk of jealousy, she concluded, was a mere pretext. 'He says [he must set] his career *avant tout*, is this the way to speak to a woman who has sacrificed everything for him?' (17 February 1834).

Bellini's side of the story is missing. There seems little doubt that he behaved ill: just as Turina needed him most, he backed off. The question is: was he not perhaps telling the truth or something close to it when he said his love had cooled? A relationship like that with Turina, which committed neither to shared lives or even to spending a great deal of time in each other's company, might well go on out of habit – until a crisis blew up and faced both of them with a choice. Its sexual side may have grown wearisome; unable to put that into words, Bellini may have fallen back on a traditional southern griev-ance like Turina's alleged 'coquetry'. She was probably right to call it a pretext: he sounds unconvinced. What is clear is that the prospect of taking her on as a lifetime companion gave him a fright. When he heard that she might come to Paris he threatened to leave the city (11 March 1834).

Embittered though she was, she went on communicating with him – but for the first few months of 1834, when she would not at one time receive letters mentioning Bellini's name. Some business mat-ters they did have to discuss, if only through a third person, for he had left money and furniture in her keeping. By July 1834 a 'most affectionate' letter from her said she still loved him but would be content with his 'cool friendship'. Bellini was tempted:

> . . . if it weren't that I have to pursue my career I would have
> decided to take up our relationship once more [he told Florimo],
> but with so many commitments in various countries, such a
> relationship would be *fatal* to me, because it would take away
> *my time* and *my peace* as well; so I'll send her an evasive note, if
> possible without hurting her (24 July 1834).

'My career *avant tout*': she had not been mistaken in seeing that as Bellini's chief motive. A separated woman whom he could never marry, liable to psychosomatic illness, would have been a drag even if he had still loved her. As it was, he swung between retrospective charges of 'coquetry', which he claimed had made him 'suffer a great deal', and admissions that he thought of her 'with regret': he could not forget her, 'but the very idea of tying myself up once more frightens me'. By October 1834 he thought he had 'got out of the fire' and wished not to fall back into it, though he would be glad of her friendship (4 August, 4 October, 30 November 1834).

The same letter to Florimo that conveyed his 'regret' about Turina announced that he was indeed at peace, thanks to not entertaining any 'amorous passion':

> I know a beautiful woman here [in Paris] who loves me extremely: for my part I can't say as much; but I find her beautiful, and kind and very docile, so much so that she gives me no trouble at all; every now and again I see her, I make love, and then I think about my opera (4 August 1834).

That was not Bellini's whole view of women – he needed a family, and at the time of writing he was seeking a wife – but it was a large part of his ideal. 'No trouble at all': Turina had never been that.

From the winter of 1834–5 Bellini was no longer obsessed with her, though he was curious about a report that she had taken an Austrian lover. This may have meant only that, like many upper-class Milanese (but unlike Pasta's circle), she was on good social terms with Austrian officers; she was in fact taken up with financial difficulties and with nursing her sick mother. She and her former lover now corresponded about his business affairs through third parties, though she once sent him a few lines, without salutation or signature. After Bellini's death she mourned him: she 'forgot everything, in order to think only of the tender affection that once bound us'. In later years she was often tired, depressed, unwell. She seems to have found a companion – a doctor who outlived her. She died in 1871.

6   Paris and death

'If you are worth one thousand, you receive one thousand; [if] one hundred thousand, one hundred thousand.' So Bellini wrote in praise of the French copyright laws (4 September 1834). In France a composer of opera could forget the losing battle with pirate managements and publishers that Italian anarchy had forced on him. Thanks to legal and administrative safeguards some of which went back before the 1789 revolution, he could be sure – provided he set a libretto in French – of collecting royalties from theatres not just in Paris but in the many provincial towns where successful operas circulated year after year. In a country with a large, musically educated bourgeoisie he could also earn well from the sale of printed music. From one work – so Bellini heard – the composer Hérold had recently made 40,000 francs, three times as much as he himself had ever earned in Italy; and he was the highest paid Italian composer. No wonder he stopped off in Paris on his way to London in late April 1833 to talk over the possibility of writing for the Opéra.

Through the remaining two and a half years of his life that was Bellini's goal. He persisted besides in an attempt, less wholehearted, to find a wife. That he managed neither, and instead scored a huge success with an opera for the Théâtre-Italien in Paris, came of the accident of death. He stubbornly pursued, through many twists, a contract with one or other of the two French-language opera houses; I puritani itself tried out his ability to please a French audience. He would no doubt have got there in the end, as Rossini and others had

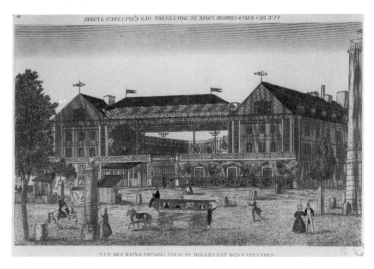

14 The Bains Chinois, where Bellini lodged when he was in Paris between 1833 and 1835. The building was painted in 'Chinese' lacquer colours. Contemporary print.

before him and as Donizetti and Verdi were to do later on. He might have got married as well.

London and Paris in the 1830s were not only the two biggest cities in Europe; they were the capitals of the two most industrialized, hence richest and most advanced countries in the world. What Bellini felt as he set eyes on them we do not know. Journalistic clichés about London, in 'fragments of letters' published by Florimo, are almost certainly fakes; in authentic letters he was content to describe it as the most magnificent and luxurious of cities. We do know that he left off composing for a year: as he explained, 'a young man in my situation, in London and Paris for the first time, could only enjoy himself immensely' (16 May, 26 June 1833, 11 March 1834). A modern equivalent might be a successful young film director from Warsaw on his first trip to Los Angeles and New York.

To an Italian musician, Paris offered a special prize. The city stood at the heart of European culture – headquarters of fashion, journalism, and gossip; a reputation made there would travel to Lisbon and

Moscow. Its language – though Bellini had trouble with it – was known to the educated throughout Europe. It was the capital of pleasure, full of tourists and well-off foreign residents who swelled the audience in theatre and concert hall. In music it pioneered the symphony orchestra; its operatic traditions were harder to crack, but the helpful copyright laws made the effort worth while. London, in contrast, offered little besides money. Its language struck most Continentals as outlandish; Bellini did not attempt it. Opera, an imported Italian luxury, managed only a four-month season; the native musical theatre veered persistently into ballad opera and pantomime, forms that the dying Weber had compromised with in *Oberon* but that Italian composers could hardly accept. Add to that the climate, the soot, the fog.

For these reasons Bellini's London stay of nearly four months – from late April to mid-August 1833 – was almost bound to be an interlude. Circumstances probably made it a disappointment as well.

He did not make all the money he had hoped for. His contract with the manager of the Italian opera, Pierre-François Laporte, promised him £400 (10,000 francs) for seeing his operas on to the stage, but Laporte was in deep financial trouble and two years later Bellini was still trying to collect half his fee. If he gave singing lessons at fancy rates to women of the nobility and gentry, as Rossini had nine years earlier, we do not know of it. True, he reported that he was continually asked out to 'balls, theatres, dinners, concerts, country houses . . . so many entertainments overwhelm me'; he knew 'the whole of London' (16 May 1833). But whereas Rossini had come to London at the height of the craze for his music, Bellini met with critical rebuff: his success was social rather than professional.

'The whole of London' did include three people who a little later were to forward Bellini's career by launching him socially in Paris as well: there Harriet, Countess Granville, a famously witty woman, was the British Ambassadress, her cousin Henry Greville an honorary attaché; her brother, the bachelor Duke of Devonshire, visited from time to time. These members of the highest Whig aristocracy liked Bellini, without perhaps thinking him much more than an 'original and agreeable' acquaintance; the words are Greville's, who saw a lot of him and described him as 'very attractive, very "*fin*", and at the same time very unsophisticated [=unspoilt] and natural'. To Bellini these aristocrats had the merit of speaking Italian: the British upper classes cultivated the language, unlike their Parisian equivalents, who expected one to speak fluent French.

With the majority who spoke only English Bellini had little to do. Three weeks after his arrival he still could not get about on his own because he knew 'neither the language nor the streets'. His lodgings in Old Burlington Street – a good address – did well while the Pastas shared them, but once the opera season was over and they had gone home he felt 'oppressed by such melancholy as was killing me: I thought myself abandoned by the whole world', so he moved in with a resident Italian musician, and soon after he went back to Paris.

The reception his operas met with might have driven him away even if August had not flagged the end of the London season, when 'everyone' departed. The prevailing musical taste ran to German music; in Italian opera, to Rossini. The *Morning Chronicle* found *Norma* unoriginal and noisy, *Capuleti* 'inferior even to *Norma*', their composer 'third-rate'. Other reviews, though less drastic, agreed in thinking Bellini an imitator with, at best, a gift for pathos. The one undoubted hit (not at the Italian opera) was a pirated *Sonnambula* in an English-language version transmogrified by the musical cobbler Henry Bishop. This was thanks to Maria Malibran's performance in the title role: her intensity carried all before it. On the first night of *Norma*, in contrast, Pasta appears to have sung out of tune; the opera then did well, but not as well as Donizetti's *Anna Bolena*, something that must have galled Bellini.[27] The critics, it seems, were blind to what was new in his work. Within a year or two, as it happened, his music would break through to lasting popularity. Meanwhile he was understandably taken with Malibran, not as a lover but as the 'angel' for whom he wished to write a new part.

In Paris Bellini looked for a contract to write an opera; he did not necessarily mean to live there. If he stayed it was for a number of reasons, among them the awkwardness of going back to Milan while Giuditta Turina was on bad terms both with him and with her husband's family. The boxholders at La Scala were as close-knit as a village: many took Turina's part, and although Bellini wrote to his publisher that he laughed at this 'absurdity' the news clearly induced him to keep away (?June 1834). A more positive ground was the attraction of Paris as a centre of the arts, something Bellini realized by late September 1833, even though his negotiations with the Opéra had for the moment failed.

The director of the Opéra, Louis Véron, had apparently tempted him on his way to London with an offer of a *prime* – a flat fee – on top of royalties. This mattered because royalties, under French law, had to be split equally with the librettist; they depended on the number of performances, which might not be great, and the large-scale works put on by the Opéra might overtax the resources of provincial theatres. For these reasons, Bellini heard, Meyerbeer's *Robert le diable* – the Opéra's great hit of the early 1830s – had earned lower royalties than had some more modest opéras-comiques. Characteristically, he held out for the best – for a *prime* no less than Rossini had earned with his Paris works. Véron, whom he met again on his return from London, refused this. For the moment there was no more to be done.

Bellini none the less chose to spend the winter in Paris. By late September he had made up his mind that his career and living with Turina were incompatible. He still hoped to reach agreement with one or other of the French-language opera houses. Meanwhile he would compose for the Théâtre-Italien, the Italian-language opera house. *Il pirata* was successfully given in October, *Capuleti* in November; negotiations seem to have begun about then, and during the winter, probably in January, Bellini signed a contract to write what would turn out to be *I puritani*.

Hence a string of new departures. Bellini plunged into Parisian salon life, found it taxing, and, after a while, turned to more raffish but more congenial society. He kept after the management of the

Opéra, and opened up another front at the Opéra-Comique. He laid siege to Rossini, the presiding deity of the Italian opera house, whose goodwill he needed if he was to succeed in an unfamiliar theatrical world. He worked at *Puritani*, with a new untried librettist who needed a great deal of schooling. He seized the chance of a contract for three operas at the San Carlo in Naples. He looked for a wife.

Bellini's social success in Paris is part of his legend. The truth is that his ventures into the salons were confined almost wholly to the winters of 1833–4 and 1834–5, each time after a big professional success (first with *Pirata* and *Capuleti*, then, from late January 1835, with *Puritani*). For the rest, he spent most of his time either in a small theatrical circle or in a suburban retreat.

He lodged at the heart of the theatre district. A Chinese bathhouse sounds disreputable. The Bains Chinois, however, was a smart private hotel with a restaurant and baths attached, hopefully pagoda-like in design; Bellini had two neat rooms there. It stood on the Boulevard des Italiens, the smart avenue for shopping and promenading and sitting in the best cafés. Two streets away were the Italian opera house and, almost facing it across the boulevard, the Opéra (the old Salle Le Peletier, which no longer exists).

Rossini lived on the top floor of the Théâtre-Italien; several of Bellini's friends and colleagues from Naples and Milan appeared there, and lodged nearby. If you turned right at the Opéra, you were in the Rue de Richelieu, where Giuditta Pasta lodged during her Paris engagements. If on the other hand you turned left on coming out of the Bains Chinois and walked a hundred yards or so along the boulevard (which here changed its name to Boulevard des Capucines), you came to the apartment house where lived a rich English Jew called Levy, a man we shall hear more of; he too was involved with the Milan opera world, knew Pasta and her circle, and spoke Italian. Bellini, in other words, spent much of his time within a tiny section of Paris, largely taken up with opera and with Italian speakers.

Thanks to Lady Granville's introduction he did follow his 'system' and go out into fashionable Paris. Since the 1830 revolution and

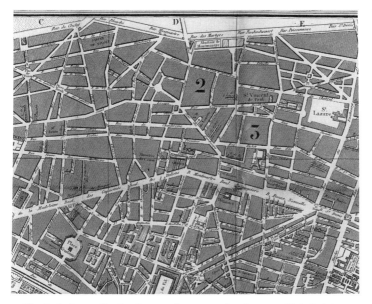

15   The Paris theatre district, from an 1830s map, showing (1) Bellini's lodging
at the Bains Chinois; (2) Levy's apartment at 9 Boulevard des Capucines; (3) the
Théâtre-Italien (Salle Favart), where Rossini lodged and Bellini's operas were
given; (4) the Opéra (Salle Le Peletier); (5) Giuditta Pasta's lodging in the Rue de
Richelieu; (6) the Opéra-Comique (Salle Ventadour). The present Opéra (Salle
Garnier) and Avenue de l'Opéra had not then been built.

the coming of the 'bourgeois king' Louis-Philippe, this meant not so
much the old royalist aristocracy as a blend of the powerful, the
newly enriched, and the artistic. Among the people who welcomed
him were the minister of the interior, Adolphe Thiers, on whose help
he counted to extract his *prime* from the management of the Opéra;
the financier Baron Sellieyre; the Italian liberal exile Princess Belgiojoso, whose salon drew leading writers and musicians; and Mme de
Flahault and Mme Jaubert, both wives of high officials, the former a
Scottish peeress in her own right. Some of the hostesses spoke Italian; most of their guests did not.

That was the trouble. Bellini never learned to speak French
with the fluency needed if he was to join in salon repartee. Several

anecdotes bear witness to his malapropisms. He once tried to ask in a shop for a felt hat (*chapeau de feutre*) and instead asked for a 'fucking-hat' (*chapeau de foutre*). On another occasion he meant to say 'That's a lie' (*bugia* in Italian), but in his French it came out as 'That's a candle' (*bougie*). According to his friend the German musician Ferdinand Hiller, Bellini's keen thought and lively feeling ensured that 'his rather muddled utterances acquired a charm, through the opposition between their content and their syntax, often lacking in the speech of the most accomplished rhetoricians', but we may doubt whether that was enough for his French hearers: Mme Jaubert's description of his speech and manner as 'childlike' suggests that he could not keep up what Parisians would regard as adult conversation. This impediment probably explains the near-total silence about Bellini the man in the many gossipy letters and diaries of the time. Once you had noted that he was good-looking and famous, there was nothing to report.

Bellini for his part found it all exhausting. In February–March 1834 he reported several times that his head was 'addled by so many carnival entertainments'; he had gone through 'a sort of *crisis*' of ill health because of all those 'soirées, balls, dinners etc. etc.' (12, 14 February, 11 March 1834). (The crisis probably came of his amoebiasis, but it felt like social indigestion.) A year later he again needed to 'call a truce to Parisian entertainments, which are fit to tire out a Hercules' (1 April, 18 May 1835). The remedy each time was to decamp to the outskirts and work there in peace.

In both 1834 and 1835 Bellini spent, or proposed to spend, nearly half the year at Puteaux, then a leafy suburb; he was there, in the house where he was to die, from just before 26 May to about 1 November 1834, and again from about 11 May 1835. He could still run into Paris for a few days at a time, for instance to rehearse *Sonnambula* at the Théâtre-Italien in October 1834: horse-drawn omnibuses left every ten minutes for central Paris and made the journey in half an hour. *Puritani*, however, he composed almost wholly at Puteaux, with the librettist visiting him when there was need.

The Puteaux house (with its servants) was put at Bellini's disposal by the tenant. This was his neighbour on the boulevard, Mr Levy. He and the woman who passed as his wife sometimes kept Bellini company, at other times went back to central Paris and let him get on with his work. As he put it, 'if we want a round of pleasure we can run [into Paris]; while here in the country we lead a peaceful, monotonous life' (30 May 1835).

Who was Levy? Who passed as Mme Levy? Because Bellini died in their care they have long roused speculation. Well before his death they were among the people he saw most of. We can now provide Levy with a near certain identity, and narrow down his mistress's to a choice of two. The evidence is complex, its unravelling laborious: it is therefore set out in an appendix suitably entitled *A detective story*. Here we will summarize the findings.

Solomon Levy was the second son of a Jewish wholesale dealer in made-up clothing who operated from a large warehouse in the East End of London. This sweated trade, based on putting out work to many individuals and small workshops at pitifully low rates, was disreputable but lucrative; Solomon's elder brother, who ran it, lived well. Solomon appears to have had little to do with the business that supported him. He was married, apparently had a house in the then fashionable suburb of Stoke Newington, but spent much time on the Continent without his wife. At some time in the early 1830s he was in Milan – perhaps as companion to a woman singer – and knew the Pastas and their circle; almost certainly he got to know Bellini there. In 1833–5 he was in his forties, possibly his late forties, and was therefore at least ten years older than Bellini. As well as playing host, he invested 40,000 francs on his friend's behalf, 30,000 of it in risky Spanish bonds; after Bellini's death he punctually returned the capital, the Spanish bonds at their then market value of 22,577.50 francs.

His mistress, whom he passed off as Mme Levy, was a theatre performer whose stage (and perhaps legal) name was Mlle Olivier. Unfortunately the evidence is not clear-cut enough to tell us whether she was Jenny Olivier, a minor singer who later was mistress to the poet Heinrich Heine, or Honorine Olivier, a dancer who in 1833 left the corps de ballet of the Opéra, where she had served since childhood and had grown up into a beautiful woman. Either would fit the facts; in 1834–5 both were about twenty-five or twenty-six, some years younger than Bellini.

A rumour current after Bellini's death made Mlle Olivier his mistress as well as Levy's. Was she perhaps the 'docile' woman whom he saw from time to time and who was 'no trouble at all', so that he could make love and then at once start thinking about his opera? At Puteaux – where Bellini was when he wrote about the woman – Mlle Olivier had ready access. If the story was true, Bellini had replicated his three-cornered arrangement with Ferdinando and Giuditta Turina: an older male friend, an intermittent affair with the friend's younger wife or mistress, and harmony among the three so long as nothing forced a showdown. What their actual relations were we cannot tell.

One thing is clear: a foreign Jew with a dubious source of income and theatrical connections, and a theatrical performer whom Turina was to describe as a 'kept woman', would not have been thought respectable by Bellini's grand acquaintances. That Bellini preferred them to the salons tells us much, first about his difficulty in keeping up polite French conversation, and secondly about his temperament. For all his dandyism and his 'system', he was more of a theatrical animal than a social climber. The Levys to him were 'kind (and good-natured)' (23 January 1835). They were, we may guess, more fun than a roomful of countesses.

Countesses and government ministers, however, had their uses, especially if they could help you to write for the Opéra. That theatre was central to Parisian and therefore to European culture. Under Véron, a doctor and entrepreneur, it was as bourgeois as the new king. Before the 1830 revolution it had cherished the austere ideals of Gluck and had carried a huge free list (accounting for about half the audience), but now it specialized in historical grand operas with ballet that were at once spectacular, educative, and exciting – more highly coloured versions of Rossini's *Guillaume Tell*; for a few years the management even made a profit.

Two obstacles stood in Bellini's way. First, everything at the Opéra and Opéra-Comique had to be in French. This gave him more trouble than it had Rossini, who cared less about words. Perhaps because of his shortcomings as a linguist, Bellini took some time to get the measure of the problem. A year went by before he remarked that a successful negotiation would mean 'writing in French, heaven help us!!'; two months later he understood that 'in order to write in French I need experience of the country and of their spirit' (21 September, 18 November 1834) – no light requirement.

The other problem was that the Opéra worked extremely slowly, on what Verdi's wife was later to call a 'system of marble and lead'. Unlike the Italian opera business, it spent months if not years on preparing, rehearsing, advertising its blockbusters. In 1834–5 it was taken up first with Halévy's *La Juive* and then with Meyerbeer's *Les Huguenots*, each a huge success. It therefore was in no hurry to commission Bellini. By March 1834 agreement seemed to him 'impossible'.

Early in August the directors of the other state theatre, the Opéra-Comique, approached him to write for them. That meant a shorter opera, with spoken dialogue and no ballet. He was keen, not just because a more accessible work would earn more money, but because the 'popular', hummable music favoured by the Opéra-Comique struck him as being 'in the Italian taste'. He would none the less meet French taste by taking particular care over finales, choruses, and concerted pieces. Like most Italians he was critical of French singers: he would have to teach them not to 'shout senselessly' or indulge in 'killing roulades'. At first he thought he had secured a contract that would give him a *prime* of 12,000 francs besides royalties, permission to recycle the music in Italy, and plenty of time to compose. It foundered on the last point: the management suddenly wanted him to catch a particular tenor who would not be available after spring 1835. That meant a rush job the moment *Puritani* was out of the way. Bellini had had enough of rush jobs; he declined (4, 21 September 1834).

Negotiations still went on intermittently into 1835. At one point
Bellini thought of adapting all his works to French texts so that they
could earn royalties and enjoy copyright protection – *Norma* at the
Opéra, the rest at the Opéra-Comique and in the provinces (Verdi
was to do that later on with some of his own Italian works). Finally,
on Rossini's advice, he resolved to try first for the Opéra, which con-
ferred prestige, and to keep the Opéra-Comique for later (10, 24
October, 18 November 1834, 18, 25 May 1835).

To the end of his life the Opéra proved elusive. There too, negotiations went on. In summer 1835 a new management still refused a
prime. Bellini, however, was playing it long. He had been discussing a
work for production in 1837, in three acts rather than the usual
mastodontic five, therefore closer to the proportions of Italian opera.
Just before his death he was willing in the last resort to do without a
prime: 'I can no longer stand being idle . . . And if the first [French
opera] is a big success, as I hope, I may be able [in future] to lay down
the law to them' (2 September 1835). Professional to the last.

Indirectly at the Opéra, and in the most direct fashion at the
Théâtre-Italien, these plans depended on the goodwill of Rossini.
With him the young newcomer had an Oedipal relation. Here all at
once was the father figure Bellini needed to win over and the rival he
must supplant.

They had met once before, in Milan in 1829; Rossini then compli-
mented Bellini to his face but, to third parties, voiced reservations he
never went back on. In 1833, when the two met again in Paris, Rossini – forty-one to Bellini's thirty-one – was morally the elder by a generation: he addressed Bellini in the intimate 'tu' while Bellini
addressed him as 'voi'.

Rossini had not composed an opera since *Guillaume Tell* four years
earlier. That work had made him a leading influence on French
opera; he was still the unquestioned god of Italian opera. We know
that in the remaining thirty-five years of his life he was never again to
write for the stage. At the time this outcome seemed increasingly
likely, because the norm was to compose year in year out. He was,

however, still free of the depression that would plague him for nearly two decades: no one could be sure that the master might not unwrap his guns and fire off another salvo.

Rossini's flat above the Théâtre-Italien symbolized his position. He did not officially run the company – that was the job of the two impresarios – but he guided its artistic policy and counselled its singers, some of them (the 'Puritani quartet' of Giulia Grisi, Rubini, Tamburini, and Lablache) among the very best ever to have been heard there. He was its 'oracle': little happened without his approval.

Looking back after the triumph of *Puritani*, which he owed in part to Rossini's guidance, Bellini wrote that to begin with the older man had been 'my worst enemy, strictly on professional grounds':

> . . . it was true [he told Florimo], absolutely true that before I approached him Rossini didn't like me at all, and he spoke ill of my music and made fun of it as much as he could, but I got on to him, I visited him often, my personality seemed attractive to him, he took to me, I asked his advice about my opera, he responded in a committed way, success came, he remained the same . . . altogether Rossini loves me' (3–4 March, 1 April 1835).

This has been taken to show Bellini's paranoia, as has a similar statement made while he was writing *Puritani*: Rossini, he knew, had set ahead of him Pacini as the most gifted young Italian composer, Donizetti as an organizer of operatic numbers, and in general puffed his own slavish imitators. Yet Bellini's account is almost certainly correct.

To Rossini, the Sicilian was the younger generation knocking at the door. Already in 1829 he had told people in Milan that *Pirata* was a very mature and accomplished work, full of feeling, but 'carried to such a pitch of philosophy that the music lacked brilliance here and there'. Such music, he told the young composer, showed that he 'must love very, very deeply', a seeming compliment he was to repeat in Paris (28 August 1829, 4 September 1834). Rossini knew, in other words, that critics had set against his own operas, allegedly over-orchestrated and cavalier in their treatment of words, Bellini's more 'philosophical' music; from such an ironist, praise for a composer's sincerity was double-edged. By 1833 Bellini had stripped down his orchestral writing still further; while still learning from Rossini about scene structure, he was moving in a new direction of his own. He had also earned – though on a rising market – fees more than twice as high as Rossini had ever got in Italy.

Rossini's 'professional' animus is understandable. Bellini might well supplant him now that the vogue had set in for a heated romanticism – a vogue the older man could not share. Bellini himself wrote that Paris judged him 'first after Rossini' (21 September 1834, 1 April 1835); as Rossini seemed to have given up opera (and was supposedly going out of fashion), that meant in practice that here too Bellini was champion. To Rossini the young composer's ambition must have been plain. No established artist likes being shouldered aside.

There were, besides, genuine artistic differences between the two. In the last year of his life Rossini inspired and provided material for a book on Bellini by a French critic. Though the author, Arthur Pougin, coarsened the result, his stress on Bellini's technical 'ignorance' and the 'monotony' and 'lack of development' in his music matches Rossini's more delicately phrased statement to Florimo. Rossini had overthrown the 'philosophical' school of Paisiello with his bolder and more elaborate writing, both vocal and instrumental, only to see it come back in a new form with Bellini. He never fully reconciled himself to it, but was too shrewd not to acknowledge the quality of the young man's music at its best.

As a childless and, like many ironists, unhappy man he was probably taken with Bellini's appeal for his goodwill – 'that of father to son, of brother to brother':

> I . . . told him [Bellini reported to Florimo] to advise me (we were alone) as brother to brother and asked him to love me; *But I do love you* (he answered). *Yes, you love me; but you must love me more* (I added). He laughed and embraced me! (4 September, 18 November 1834).

Bellini was at first minded to 'await developments and see whether he's telling the truth or not', never quite shook off his doubts, but on the whole valued Rossini's advice and came to feel that the older man sincerely meant to help – an outcome creditable to both.[28] It could happen only because they were not direct competitors. About an active rival like Donizetti, whose *Marino Faliero* came on at the Théâtre-Italien just after *Puritani* and with less success, Bellini was to begin with fearful and then scathingly dismissive.

'[Rossini] thought he could tell me something about instrumentation.' His advice helped to persuade Bellini that in composing for a French audience he needed a richer, more varied orchestral palette, but it was not the only influence at work. Paris, as Bellini came to realize, was given over to orchestral music; French composers were good at it even when their vocal writing was weak: 'as in Germany, they study effects for the orchestra and how to keep it well nourished' (1 July 1835). Already in Naples – we have seen – he had been familiar with symphonic scores, but now he could hear them performed. In London he heard Mendelssohn conduct his Italian Symphony. After hearing Beethoven's Pastoral Symphony played by the Paris Conservatoire orchestra he called out to his friend Hiller in a jumble of French and Italian '"It's as beautiful as nature" . . . and his eyes shone as if he had himself done a mighty deed.'

A further inducement to fill out and vary his orchestration was that he could no longer rely on his gift for setting Italian words. 'In Paris', he wrote, 'you need music before anything else – they don't know the [Italian] language, and they don't care whether the words are good or bad' (25 March 1835). Finally, if he was to write for the Opéra he must show that he could handle on a large scale not just the orchestra but the chorus and the forces of history, arrayed by the libretto into an edifying spectacle. Going to Paris had taken Bellini out of a self-sufficient Italian musical culture; if he was to succeed he must once again raise his game.

The result was *I puritani*, such a hit as to become the quintessential Victorian opera. 'Our dear *Puritani*' was indeed Queen Victoria's favourite; even at the height of the Wagner craze Bernard Shaw, musically trained in the 1860s, could shift his point of view 'back to that of the elderly gentlemen who still ask for nothing better than . . . a quartet of Italian singers capable of doing justice to "A te o cara"'. *Puritani* then dated badly; in recent years it has come back as a work full of life, musical life especially, though a flawed dramatic structure and the mark on it of a transitional work – a bridge from Bellini's Italian past to the French opera he wished to write – make it less perfect than *Sonnambula* or *Norma*.

British history of the Tudor and Stuart period was a fertile source of French romantic drama, in part thanks to the vogue for Scott's novels, in part because it was full of lurid incident safely removed in time. *Puritani* stemmed from a boulevard play about roundheads and cavaliers, so dense with politics and intrigue that a whole chunk had to be left out. What remained – the hero's helping the incognita Queen Henrietta Maria to escape, so driving his Puritan fiancée out of her mind – was at once insufficient and, at crucial points, absurd: after Elvira goes mad, the drama treads water until the final crisis and reconciliation; the action depends on such brainwaves as her putting her veil on an unknown woman's head, and her father's going off on a pretext just before the wedding.

Bellini none the less thought this subject – chosen by April 1834 – held 'profound interest, situations that keep the mind in suspense and lead it to feel for the suffering of innocent people': here was the pathos he had looked for in *Beatrice*, with the advantage that it sprang not from the acts of villains but from 'fate' (11 April 1834). He later owned that some of the words were poor, but he still thought the situations 'theatrical', varying pathos (as in *Sonnambula* and, behind it, in Paisiello's *Nina*) with 'military robustness' and 'puritanical austerity' (4 October 1834, 1 July 1835). Like his Italian contemporaries, he still thought in operatic numbers – apt for particular singers, and each embodying a distinct emotion; he did not look at the music drama as a whole. According to Pierluigi Petrobelli, who first defined these poetics, 'there may sometimes emerge' in Italian operas of Bellini's day 'a sense of musical unity' (as, we might add, in *Norma* and *Sonnambula*), but it is 'not . . . the result of a conscious and careful search'. While he was writing *Puritani* Bellini had too many other concerns to allow even an unconscious search.

His librettist was a political exile and minor poet who wrote song texts for composers but knew nothing of the theatre. Count Carlo Pepoli's liberalism and nationalism troubled Bellini slightly; his inexperience, a great deal.

Bellini was a pre-Risorgimento figure, neither a liberal nor an Italian nationalist and fundamentally unconcerned with politics. True, when he decided to stay on in Paris he still wished to keep his hand in as a composer for Italian theatres. As he pursued a contract for the San Carlo, Naples, that would further raise his standard fee he sent his friend Lamperi a statement for public consumption: though Paris was good for his career Lamperi must not

> think I am giving up my beloved Italy; she has seen me grow, has fed me, and my mother is there and I am very attached to my family, so she will always be dear to me, very dear, so much so that if . . . I am unable to go [to Naples] to see my opera on to the stage I will send it, but I will never give up writing for my country unless when I no longer compose for any theatre. This secret you may reveal to everyone (12 February 1834).

It was a public relations exercise: later, when managements in both Naples and Milan – 'these imbeciles' – declined to meet his fees Bellini threatened to stop writing for Italy; whatever he wrote for French theatres would be deliberately unfitted to Italian conditions. This time he asked his correspondent – Florimo – to tell no one, so he was just blowing off steam (4 August 1834). We need not conclude that Italy meant nothing to him. It was bound up with his family and with the world of music; it called up in him the feelings of a child, whether attached or disaffected, but that was all.

Pepoli, on the other hand, had taken part in a liberal revolution in Bologna; he shared the yearning of his friend the great poet Leopardi for an Italy nobly independent. With *Puritani* he seized his chance. A tale of the English Civil War could show a 'people rightly struggling to be free', a notion anyhow welcome to a Paris audience in the 1830s. He proposed a hymn to liberty, to follow the opening chorus. Bellini pointed out that you could not have two martial choruses in a row, spoke of moving the hymn to a later scene, and in the end, when he needed to give the two basses more to do, turned it into the cabaletta to the duet 'Il rival salvar tu dêi'; there it did not make the best of sense but, as 'Suoni la tromba', became the hit of the opera.

His attitude was pragmatic. The hymn was 'only for Paris, where they like ideas of liberty'; for Naples, where he hoped to recycle the opera, every liberal word would be either changed or cut out; the very title *Puritani* could go (26 May, 10 October, 21 November 1834). As he worked on 'Suoni la tromba' he told Florimo that it was '*liberal* enough to give one a fright' (5 January 1835); to Pepoli he wrote, probably on the same day, 'the sound of trumpets will cause all free hearts in the theatre to quiver with joy. Farewell. – Long live liberty.'

Again, we need not think him insincere. He tackled Pepoli with a mixture of cajolery, bullying, and joshing; 'long live liberty' was a humorous concession to the man he called 'Doctor Carluccio', 'Pepolic genius', 'hard little head', just as, in London, he had humoured the liberal authoress Lady Morgan by playing and singing for her a hymn in praise of Italy, 'white, red, and green as a flower' (the tricolour of Napoleon's kingdom). Such gestures cost nothing.

Pepoli's inexperience gave Bellini plenty to cope with: the poet held to the 'rules', his dialogue to begin with was at once 'prolix', unclear, and short of passion, and his diction was at times poor (c. April, 30 May, c. September 1834, 18 May 1835). Looking back nearly forty years later, Pepoli recalled that Bellini had been kind but 'eccentric':

> At times he called me *an angel, a brother, a saviour*; and at times, on his changing the melodies and the music for the third or fourth time, and my remarking how difficult or impossible it was to

change the structure of the drama or the verses, he fell into a rage, calling me *man without* a heart, without friendship or feeling: and then we would again become great friends, better than ever.

Bellini cut out some of Pepoli's verses and made him rewrite others. He still let through a tongue-twister like 'cui cinser tue rose' – something Romani would not have perpetrated. Nor could he impose his own words as Verdi was to do.

Lack of a definitive text bedevils *Puritani* more than any of Bellini's other works. Possibilities abound.

The opera was to have served as one of three he had undertaken to write for Naples, in a version adapted for Maria Malibran and other singers: hence transpositions and the building up of the soprano's part at the end instead of the tenor's. Bellini sent this off during the Paris rehearsals, in a rush to beat the Naples deadline and the quarantine imposed by cholera in the south of France. (In the event it was held up just long enough to miss the deadline and give the financially troubled Naples management an excuse to break the contract.) Then, because the opera threatened to run well past the 11 p.m. curtain time set by police regulations, he made cuts in the Paris score just before and after the first night. These did away with expansive sections of several concerted pieces; they can, however, be retrieved from the Naples score. A seeming blemish, the ludicrously swift reprieve and final curtain (still found at Covent Garden in 1992), comes of such a cut – one Bellini particularly deplored; it can now be avoided.[29]

Cut or not, *Puritani* overflows with music. In his retreat at Puteaux Bellini had plenty of time. The first night was delayed from November 1834 until 25 January 1835, in part because of Pepoli's slowness, but the schedule was less tight than that of a season in Italy: the composer was not rushed. Four great singers demanded and offered rich opportunities. The first night brought an 'explosion' of enthusiasm; it left Bellini 'shaking . . . at times stunned'; *Puritani* was the talk of the town, the king and queen invited Bellini, and the minister Thiers made him a knight of the Legion of Honour.

16 One of Ferri's original sets for *I puritani*. The print exaggerates its height and width.

Puritani is, in Alfred Einstein's words, 'a kind of grand opera'. Bellini uses offstage instruments, chorus, and soloists to evoke a far-away time and place: *Norma's* Gaul might be anywhere, any time, but we are in history – that, rather than the exact location (Plymouth), is the point. The opening horn calls, spaced out in changing measures, the rapt offstage prayer, the brilliant martial chorus all evoke a climate of austerity and war. In the last act the troubadour's song – sung, again offstage, by the crazed Elvira and then onstage by Arturo – is a grand opera device, part ornamental, part evocative of a distant era. Yet, for all the mentions of Cromwell and Parliament, history scarcely matters. What shapes the work towards grand opera is its combination of spectacle, brilliance, and romance, achieved in part by careful scoring for orchestra and chorus, in part by spatial devices like offstage sounds; Bellini had come a long way since the crude echo effects in *Pirata*.

More offstage voices build up to the opera's two key scenes, first to the tenor's Act 1 entrance and the ensemble 'A te o cara', an extraordinary Bellinian flowering from the initial rising fourth and lilting rhythm through an undulant melodic line to a seemingly endless climax, the high note, as Berlioz wrote at the time, 'hovering above the deep notes and ornaments of [the two basses], arranged so as to produce slight passing dissonances against the upper pedal' – an 'admirable effect'; we might add: a glimpse of heaven.

Again, Elvira's voice as she wanders about the recesses of the castle opens what Bellini variously called a trio, an aria, and a scena, 'Qui la voce sua soave' – really an equivalent to Ophelia's mad scenes, framed and distanced by the sorrowing comments of baritone and bass. Against contemporary practice, it begins offstage with the heartrending climax ('O rendetemi la speme') of Elvira's andantino melody; the full melody is stated only as she comes on. Fragments of her vocal line (here and there taken over or supported by the men) are distributed along its orchestral version, which is continuous but irregular, never exactly repeated. The orchestra's subtly varied rise and fall speaks for unending sorrow, the vocal fragments for the discontinuity in Elvira's mind; the moment when she fancies she is getting married – allegro giusto, a reminiscence of the betrothal chorus in Act 1 – makes a faintly tinny, ghostly interlude, and the rising cascades of semitones in the cabaletta ('Vien diletto') use coloratura to show the final sideslip into hysteria. In this astonishing scene Bellini works his melodic gift at its most poignant while he bends the structures of Italian opera to create music drama.

Sorrow frozen yet transfigured is the note of 'Credeasi, misera!', the slow section of the Act 3 concertato, another distinguished number that works by quiet means – the peak of the melodic curve rises each time by a tone or semitone; it combines 'amplitude, rich sonority, clarity, and formal concision' (Lippmann). The baritone's Act 1 aria ('Ah! per sempre io ti perdei'), the bass's Act 2 aria with chorus ('Cinta di fiori'), and the opening section of their duet ('Il rival salvar

17 Giulia Grisi as Elvira and Luigi Lablache as Giorgio in the original
production of *I puritani*. Contemporary print.

G. B. RUBINI NELL'OPERA I PURITANI.

18 G. B. Rubini as Arturo in I puritani, a part written to exploit his very high range.

tu dêi') are characteristic legato melodies moving within a small range to eloquent and original effect. The two hits of the show in 1835 – the polacca 'Son vergin vezzosa', written with Malibran's fiery delicacy in mind, and the warlike 'Suoni la tromba' – were both dismissed by Berlioz as trivial. Such trivialities keep an opera on the boards when graver works disappear: a brilliant coloratura showpiece (apt to Elvira's excited state) and a vigorous march, so irresistible as to cancel out the nonsense of the two men's hoping to kill Arturo in battle when, a few minutes earlier, one was begging the other to save him.

That is the kind of thing that makes *Puritani*, for all its riches and fluency, a less satisfying whole than *Norma* or *Sonnambula*. Bellini and Romani, working side by side in optimum conditions, could after all bring off more than a string of well-contrasted numbers. Whether or not the composer saw the theoretical possibility, in practice he achieved two coherent works of art. In *Puritani*, with an inexpert librettist he could not fully control, and with one eye to an unaccustomed form, he slipped at times into the bane of grand opera, what Wagner was to call 'effects without causes'. It is nevertheless a feast of music studded with effective scenes, among them two or three of transcendent beauty; the brighter, fuller orchestral writing on which Bellini took such pains enhances the sense of Victorian profusion; it remains exhilarating.

Though tending towards the grand French style, *Puritani* was an Italian opera, marketable throughout Europe. From the Paris production Bellini earned, it seems, only a little more than he had been getting in Italy for a new work; but as he composed he negotiated for productions elsewhere, not only of the 'Malibran' version in Naples but of the Paris version in Milan and Palermo, and for the publishing rights in Milan and Naples, all of which should have brought in handsome sums; the Paris impresarios were looking to hire out the score to other Italian theatres.

With the Naples management, a group of upper-class amateurs, Bellini bargained by post from February to November 1834. He ended by accepting a package deal that would have given him just over 13,000 francs for each of three new operas – little more than his previous record, but as one of the three was the recycled *Puritani* he could still consider himself champion. It meant spending 'fifteen sleepless nights' to get *Puritani* revised, copied, and dispatched – as we have seen, in vain.

Soon after hearing that the Naples management had seized the occasion to break the contract, Bellini found that all the other deals were off as well. Pirates had struck: Italian managements and publishers already had the score – no mere counterfeit but an authentic copy. Only just before his last illness did Bellini discover the culprit: the chief copyist of the Théâtre-Italien, Cesare Pugni, a penniless composer who had fled from his Milan creditors. Bellini had paid him as copyist, passed on to him some nearly new clothes, recommended him as a teacher, and slipped him the odd five-franc piece. 'It will be a lesson to me', he wrote; were it not for Pugni's six innocent children 'I should like to ruin him' (2, 3 September 1835).

Bellini was not ruined, but he had lost potential fees running into tens of thousands of francs. While he was still bargaining with Naples he had told Florimo that, the chance of writing for Malibran apart, money was his chief concern:

> . . . now that I no longer need to win fame one must think, up to a point, of one's own financial interests; [one must] not be an ass and run the risk of finding oneself short of a fair independence once talent runs out (13 October 1834).

The next sentence in this letter announced that he was writing to Giuditta Pasta to bring up once again his old notion of marrying her daughter Clelia. One way to achieve a 'fair independence' – at that time thoroughly respectable, indeed desirable in middle-class eyes – was to marry money. Bellini actively pursued it through most of his Paris stay. If he succeeded, he pointed out, he could write at leisure for the French opera houses.

That did not mean that he would marry just anybody. Bellini's

19 A late portrait of Bellini, by Julien.

search for a wife has drawn sarcasm, in part because of twentieth-century incomprehension of earlier attitudes, in part because critics have accepted as genuine a nastily worded letter that is one of Florimo's concoctions – if not a fake, at least altered and in part made up.[30] Bellini himself, in a long, authentic letter, owned that his search might appear ridiculous. He none the less set out his hopes:

> To have for my own a young girl, pretty and well brought up,
> will lead me no longer to have any relationships with women who
> are not mine, which bring continual ill-feeling. As for my wife
> (supposing her too to be inclined to flirt), I am the master: I will
> receive whom I please, I will take her travelling if the fancy takes
> me, etc. etc.: yet I don't think I shall be compelled to such
> measures; I know myself: if I marry a woman who is agreeable and
> good-looking, and kind as well, I believe I shall keep her company
> as affectionately as can be: now women, all of them without
> exception, behave ill to their husbands only when they are
> neglected; so for the moment I am imagining a happy state . . .
> (30 November 1834)

This was sincere. That a bride should ideally be young, devoted, obedient, and bring a solid dowry was the agreed norm. Bellini's expectations were if anything less crass than those of many male contemporaries, who would not have ruled out extra-marital affairs.

Candidates were, to start off with, close to his old friend and chief interpreter Giuditta Pasta. One of the first people Bellini met in Paris was a young Englishwoman to whom Pasta had sent him. Charlotte Hunloke was a baronet's sister, member of an old Roman Catholic gentry family from Lancashire that now lived just outside Paris; she spoke Italian as well as French. When Hunloke was about eighteen Pasta had for a year or two entrusted her with the care of her daughter; the point was to keep Clelia away from the world of the theatre. In spring 1834 Bellini proposed, but Hunloke replied that she felt only esteem and friendship; he felt no more; her age (about twenty-five) meant that if she did not love him she would be too old to bend to his habits or to his mode of feeling; her brother would give her only 150,000 francs (an income of £300 a year) and '150,000 francs without love isn't much'. He was also put off by her teeth (11 March, 30 November 1834). The truth was that her heart was committed, obsessively committed – to Pasta; for the singer she felt lifelong 'idolatry' (her term), and even after the death of Bellini (who had given her a lock of his hair) nearly all she could write about was his devotion to Pasta.

In October 1834 Bellini 'revived' his interest in Clelia Pasta. Her father's reply was 'most polite but icy'. Bellini later thought the parents might have been influenced by sympathy with Giuditta Turina (30 November 1834, 13 August 1835). He did not realize how determined Giuditta Pasta was that Clelia should have nothing to do with theatre people. Both Pastas had gone on the stage to repair the fortunes of 'good' families that had suffered in the Napoleonic wars. If they countenanced Bellini's interest three years earlier – and he may have misunderstood them – it was no doubt because he, like Pasta herself, hoped to make a lot of money and retire early. They now hastened to marry Clelia off to a cousin.

Once these two possibilities vanished the wife of his rich friend Baron Sellieyre proposed an eighteen-year-old girl who would have 200,000 francs and who no doubt spoke Italian – a daughter of the successful painter Horace Vernet, director of the French School in Rome. It was this proposal that set Bellini 'imagining a happy state', but when he met the girl she turned out to be 'too lively', and too intent on having her own way; a few months later she married someone else.

There was still Baron Sellieyre's niece, 'rather pretty, sweet-tempered, of good family . . . full of religion and good principles and very well bred'. Bellini felt confident enough to write about her to his own family in Catania; this meant that he was serious. The trouble was that she had little money, while he would marry no one with less than 200,000 francs: the resulting income of 10,000 francs (£400) a year and a good wife would make him 'independent of everybody and everything'. Might her uncle not give her a dowry? (30 November 1834, 1 April, 18 July 1835).

That is the last we hear of Bellini's plans. He himself owned that he was in two minds about marriage and tended to lose interest once the prospect drew near. We may guess at an uncertain sexual identity, or at a clash between his conventional expectation of a young, untried wife and his need for an accepting, semi-maternal figure. All the same, his persistence suggests that if he had lived he would have got married, just as he would probably have composed a French opera. What either would have led to we cannot know.

In early June 1834 he suffered from what he thought might be gastric fever, but was soon well again. There is no sign of a recurrence in the early summer of 1835. A notorious episode in Mme Jaubert's drawing-room took place about then. Heine teased Bellini by saying that geniuses were supposed to die young, particularly between thirty and thirty-five, so he was at risk; Bellini was perturbed and made the Italian sign (the index and little finger pointed) against the evil eye. Heine, who disliked Bellini's rosiness and physical bloom, was indulging his 'satanic' manner; any southern Italian might have responded as Bellini did. On 24 July Bellini wrote that his health was excellent; he was, however, worried by cholera in Provence and on the Riviera, which might spread to the rest of France and Italy. Only on 2 September did he write 'I have been slightly troubled for three days by a diarrhoea.' His last known letter is dated the next day. On 11 September he told a visitor that he was suffering from 'a slight dysentery' but expected to recover shortly. He died less than a fortnight later, on 23 September at 5 p.m.

We know what he died of: the autopsy report described the symptoms thoroughly even though amoebic infection was not then understood as a specific illness. An abscess had formed on his liver, the size of a fist, that could soon have burst; what killed him were, however, other results of the amoebiasis – loss of blood from multiple ulceration of the large intestine, and loss of water from dysentery.

20 Neapolitan print commemorating Bellini's death, 1835. Each of the rays
fanning out from the lyre bears the title of one of his operas.

That apart, all we know of his last illness comes from two sources:
brief notes from an Italian doctor, Luigi Montallegri, who treated
Bellini from 9 or 10 September; and extracts from the diary of a
young friend, Auguste Aymé – the visitor who saw him at Puteaux on
11 September, tried in vain to see him on the 12th and 13th, and, on
the afternoon of the 23rd, walked into the house to find Bellini dead.

Much nonsense has been written about these two. It was the holiday season, when many well-off people were away from Paris, among them, no doubt, some fashionable doctors. Montallegri was an experienced ex-army doctor; his remedy – cupping – was orthodox though useless; he saw Bellini on each of the last four days and, on the 23rd, proposed to spend all day and all night with him. It is idle to suppose that a more eminent doctor would have done better.

Auguste Aymé – accounted for in detail in the Appendix – was a nineteen-year-old man about town, nephew of the Neapolitan aristocrat Michele Carafa (a composer who had settled in Paris and who wrote for the Opéra-Comique). Contrary to what biographers have written, Aymé had no official position. His diary extracts seem plausible but have to be taken on trust. According to him, the lady of the house – Mme Levy, or Mlle Olivier – came in while he was visiting Bellini on the 11th and complained 'sharply' that the sick man needed absolute rest; Aymé took the hint and left. On subsequent days, the gardener turned him and the composer Mercadante away, saying that no one was allowed in; Carafa got in on the 14th by pretending to be a doctor, and found Bellini greatly agitated. By the 22nd Bellini's friends in the opera world were alarmed at the quarantine and talked of getting a magistrate to intervene. Early on the morning of the 23rd Aymé was again turned away; when he came back in the afternoon through a downpour he pushed open the gate and found the house temporarily empty but for Bellini's corpse; the gardener, who had gone out to summon people and buy candles, told him that the Levys had left for Paris but did not say when.

The Levys and Dr Montallegri probably feared that Bellini might have cholera. An epidemic – we have seen – threatened from the south. The disease was known to be contagious, though the means of contagion was not understood. To have on one's hands the first cholera case in the area would be troublesome; it made sense to isolate the patient, hope for the best, and say as little as possible. This at any rate seems a reasonable explanation.

As for the Levys' having decamped (perhaps after the patient had lost consciousness), Bellini had chosen to live with somewhat raffish people on the fringe of the opera world. They were, as he said, kind, they were no doubt fun, and if Mlle Olivier was the occasional mistress who gave 'no trouble' they provided him with satisfaction all round. That they should wobble at the crisis followed from the rest.

Though keen for an 'independence', Bellini was to the end faithful to the world of lyric theatre he had grown up in, and almost entirely faithful to its ideals. Those ideals were of clarity, grace, and austere expression of feeling through the word set to music. They were rooted in a pre-revolutionary musical culture, innocent of the great nineteenth-century themes of History, Liberty, Nature, and the People. Only in *Puritani* did Bellini tentatively pick up those themes; even there he all but drowned them in music.

In his mature works his gift for original, distinguished, unforgettable melody – a gift exceedingly rare – went together with an intensification of sonority and a poignancy of feeling his late eighteenth-century forebears had not dreamt of. We cannot tell how he would have developed if he had lived a full span. As it was his achievement was unique, and is enough.

Appendix

A detective story: the rentier, the kept woman, and the young man about town

If we are to understand how Bellini lived and died in his last phase in Paris, we need to know the identities of three people:

1 the English Jew S. Levy, his friend and near neighbour on the boulevard, in whose house at Puteaux Bellini died after having spent (or planned to spend) about five months of each year there (from sometime before 26 May 1834 to late October 1834, and from about 11 May 1835 to his death on 23 September 1835); sometimes referred to as Lewis, and sometimes spelt Levis, Levys, or Lewys;

2 Levy's 'wife', referred to as Mme Levy but almost certainly not his legal wife; known as Mlle Olivier to

3 Auguste Aymé, a young friend of Bellini's, our only witness to the composer's dying days (apart from Dr Montallegri, whose evidence is strictly medical).

Finding out involves something like detective work. Let us take the last of these persons first.

I. Auguste Aymé
His diary entries from 11 to 23 September 1835 (transcribed by him in 1880 and communicated to Francesco Florimo, who published them)[31] are the crucial source for Bellini's friends having been kept out of the house where he lay ill and dying, and for the Levys' seemingly strange behaviour. Aymé has been described by all biographers since 1935 as Baron Aymé d'Aquino, 'plenipotentiary' (sometimes

'attaché') in the Paris legation of the Kingdom of the Two Sicilies; some have written indignantly of so important a personage being denied access. Who was he?

In 1835 he was neither baron nor d'Aquino, nor was he as yet a diplomat; when he became one, it was (as Florimo stated) in the French service (making him a representative of the Two Sicilies was an error by Francesco Pastura in his 1935 edition of Bellini's letters,[32] followed by later biographers).

Auguste-Louis-Victor Aymé, born on 25 April 1816, was the son of Lieutenant-General Charles-Jean-Louis Aymé – a Frenchman, a baron of the Empire whose career had survived the Restoration, and a landowner near Melle in the Deux-Sèvres department – and of a Neapolitan noblewoman, sister of the composer Michele Carafa. Carafa had himself been an officer in Napoleon's army and in 1806 had moved with his family to Paris; in 1835 he was still living there and was active as a composer, chiefly of opéra-comique. Young Aymé entered the French diplomatic service, even then as an unpaid attaché, only in November 1836.[33] He was not made a baron (with the additional surname d'Aquino) until 1845.[34] At the time of Bellini's death in September 1835, therefore, he was a mere young man about town, aged nineteen, and untitled.

His diary entries show that he was in touch with his uncle Carafa and with other people in the opera world, as well as with Bellini. It is reasonable to suppose that he already had the *entrées* to the dancers' green room at the Opéra (foyer de la danse), a well-known meeting-place for women dancers and their admirers; in 1854, when for an unknown reason the *entrées* were taken away from him, he had had them for some time.[35] We may also suppose that he was familiar with the backstage area of the Théâtre-Italien and the Opéra-Comique. But he had no position such as to impress the Levys or their servants.

Aymé's later diplomatic career was mediocre. It took him over three years and several petitions to become a paid attaché, seven and a half more years (and more petitions) to become *aspirant diplomatique*. His family's friendship with Queen Marie-Amélie (Louis-Philippe's Neapolitan wife) seems to have been of little help, but their Napoleonic connections paid off when Louis-Napoleon made him a second secretary in 1850, and first secretary in 1854. In all these grades he served in European capitals (Naples, Hanover, Hamburg, Berne, Lisbon, Turin, St Petersburg), with intervals in Paris. He did not become head of mission (at Tangier) until 1864. After the fall of Napoleon III he was sent on indefinite leave in 1871 and retired on a pension in 1876. He then lived in Naples, where he died on 31 January 1889, leaving a widow.

Aymé's very mediocrity, and his having done nothing to exploit the Bellini myth apart from communicating his diary entries to Florimo, suggest that the entries are reliable. We do, however, depend utterly on his word: the whereabouts of the diary is unknown and there appear to be no descendants. For what it is worth, the entries do not read like fakes worked up long after the event; they seem spontaneous.

II. S. Levy

That is how he signed himself in a letter (in the Museo Belliniano), addressed to Bellini's father after the composer's death; in it he described Bellini as his 'dear friend and brother' and as 'part of my family'.[36] The flourish at the end of the signature could possibly be read as an 's' and the whole as S. Levys. Bellini and Rossini, however, who both knew him, wrote his name Levy in those letters whose originals can be checked. The man himself, in two business letters sold at Sotheby's on 1 December 1995 (part of a mass of papers concerning Bellini's funeral), signed one of them clearly 'S. Levy'; the other shows the familiar ambiguous flourish.

What did the initial 'S' stand for? Modern biographies say Samuel. This name originates in the 1935 catalogue of the Museo Belliniano,[37] which, however, spells the surname Lewys (certainly not what appears in the letter), and lists no other letter by him; it misspells many other names. In the absence of documentary proof, we must take it that 'S' need not stand for Samuel.

As for 'Lewis' and its variants, Levy was sometimes referred to by that name, for instance, in 1835, by Bellini's friend Pietro Ponzani, a lawyer and a member of Giuditta Pasta's circle, who had known him in Milan; at that time Levy/Lewis still owed Ponzani a small sum – 160 francs.[38] For this there could be two explanations: like some other English Jews he had adopted the surname Lewis;[39] or he had to do with someone called Lewis. Given the use of Levy by people who knew him well, the latter seems the more probable; in Milan he may have been connected with the British soprano Marianna Lewis, who was in Italy at least from 1827 to 1831. Marianna had studied with Pasta in Paris and went on to study with Banderali in Milan. She sang at La Scala in carnival 1828, at the San Carlo, Naples, in 1831, and had an abortive engagement in Venice in between, but she appears to have had little success; Bellini in 1831 thought her 'less than mediocre' and would not have her in his operas.[40] After that date no more is heard of her. Levy's connection with Marianna – as relative or lover – is hypothetical. His stay in Milan is not: it would in any case have enabled him to meet Bellini (who was based in Milan from April 1827 to December 1832) in Pasta's circle.

We are therefore looking for an English Jew called S. Levy, sometimes referred to as Lewis, who was living in Paris in 1834/5 but made a short trip to London in the spring of 1835;[41] who had been known in Milan operatic circles not long before; who spoke and wrote Italian but not quite correctly; was well off; rented a luxurious flat at 9 Boulevard des Capucines[42] as well as a largish house at 19bis Rampe du Pont de Neuilly, Puteaux; who had a box at the Italian opera and knew Rossini;[43] and whose 'wife' was known to Aymé as Mlle Olivier.

Besides this, we know that he invested on Bellini's account nearly 30,000 francs in Spanish bonds – a highly risky investment because of the civil war then going on – as well as 10,000 francs laid out more conservatively at 5 per cent. But it does not follow that – as some have concluded – Levy was a banker: to invest the money he need only go to one of the many Paris brokers, official and unofficial. Why did Bellini not go to a broker himself? Probably because the Paris financial world was strange to him. Bellini's alarm as Spanish bonds lost half their value reflects not on Levy but on the speculative greed he had shared with many people in Paris (a mainspring of the plot in Dumas's The Count of Monte-Cristo, published nine years after Bellini's death). In the event Levy behaved impeccably: right after Bellini's death he paid the heirs the 10,000 francs, with interest, and, a little later, 22,577.50 francs on account of the Spanish bonds, which had recovered somewhat.[44]

That is all. At first glance, looking for an S. Levy is as daunting an enterprise as finding a J. Smith. His wealth, however, rules out the many men called S. Levy in contemporary London Jewish records and street directories who were small traders and craftsmen. One can then concentrate on the genealogies of a handful of well-off families. An exhaustive search of available genealogies brings forward just one person who fits the circumstances: we cannot prove that he is the man, but we can be reasonably sure.[45]

This is Solomon Levy, 'of Stoke Newington and Paris', second son of Michael Abraham Levy, 'gentleman', and younger brother of Abraham Levy, an affluent merchant; both his father and his brother were partners in Moses, Levy & Co. The crucial point about this family is that their business – carried on since at least 1810 – was as wholesale 'slopsellers' in the East End of London: they sold ready-made clothing.

In the early nineteenth century, anyone with pretensions had clothes made for them. The 'slop end' of the trade was cheap and based on putting out work to many sweatshops and to individuals, notoriously low paid, who worked from home; it boomed with the growth in population and in the numbers of people who could now afford more than one suit of clothes. The business was at first carried on at 21 Nightingale Lane, then, from 1826 at the latest, at 2 and 3 Aldgate. From 1879 Moses, Levy & Co. were listed as 'merchants' with an address at 6 Fenchurch Street, nearer the heart of the City; the Aldgate premises were at that time occupied by an Army clothier.

Wholesaling cheap clothes from a warehouse in Aldgate could make you rich. Solomon's father, the 'gentleman', who died in 1828, lived near the shop, in Little Alie Street, but the elder son, Abraham, 'did very comfortably' in Finsbury Square, then a good residential address. Abraham, aged sixty-six at his death in 1848, had been born in 1781 or 1782. Though we have no dates for Solomon, we may presume him to have been born sometime in the later 1780s. That would make him, in 1834–5 when he and Bellini spent much time together, about forty-five to fifty – some twelve to seventeen years older than the composer.

Solomon was married to Kitty Joseph; their daughter Sarah married one Picard, perhaps a French or Swiss Jew (several Picards worked in the Paris opera world, but not enough is known to identify any of them as Solomon's son-in-law).[46] Stoke Newington, where Solomon apparently lived some of the time, was, in the 1830s, an 'eminently respectable' suburb, with 'numerous handsome detached residences'.[47] Kitty, we may suppose, either died young or stayed behind, a grass widow in Stoke Newington, while Levy amused himself on the Continent. There is no sign of his doing any work. He was presumably a rentier or remittance man, living off the wholesale clothing trade back home.[48]

III. Mlle Olivier

That 'Mme Levy' was Levy's mistress, not his wife, is shown by two pieces of evidence. Aymé, after meeting her in Bellini's sickroom, wrote 'Mme Lewis, whom I knew under the name of Mlle Olivier . . .' This might be taken for a mention of an ordinary bourgeois woman if it were not for the second piece of evidence. Giuditta Turina, after Bellini's death, feared that some jewellery she had given her former lover might have fallen into the hands of 'that dreadful kept woman'.[49] It is difficult to see whom she could have meant other than the mistress of the house where Bellini died. How did Giuditta know? Either Bellini, who was still writing to her (letters she probably destroyed), had told her; or he told Florimo, who was in touch with Giuditta and passed on the information.

Mlle Olivier was most likely a member of the opera world. The obvious place for a young man of Aymé's connections to have met her was an operatic green room. It was also an obvious place for Levy to have got to know her on his return from Milan.

Was she a singer or a dancer? If she had been a singer of any ability one might have expected Bellini to mention it in surviving letters (which refer to her now and then, neutrally but for a mention of her and Levy's 'good-heartedness'). She could, however, have been one of the many in Paris who got by on looks, verve, and a modest voice; Bellini thought nothing of them. Dancers, especially members of the corps de ballet at the Opéra, were notorious as apprentice courtesans. The foyer de la danse was where they met rich men, ministers, ambassadors, peers, princes of the blood. According to the director of the Opéra in 1830–5, their mothers 'train them up early to all the devices of coquetry and . . . teach them only the art of being beautiful and giving pleasure'; every now and then one of them would leave the company to be kept in luxury by a new protector.[50] We will look at all contemporary Mlles Olivier in the theatrical profession.

This can be done through the theatrical press and the archives of the Opéra.[51] It is a long job, made difficult by the contemporary habit of billing performers as 'Mme' or 'Mlle' without a Christian name, and by the number of theatre people called Olivier; the surname is fairly common, but it may have been popular as a stage name as well. On the other hand the press sometimes gave performers' home addresses, so making them easier to trace.

The following are potential candidates among singers:

1 Mlle Olivier, rising actress (and perhaps singer) at the Ambigu-Comique, 1821–7 until the fire that destroyed that theatre; at the Gaîté, 1829; not heard of afterwards;

2 Jenny [Caroline] Olivier, singer-actress at Vaudeville, 1829; Théâtre de la Banlieue, 1829 (leading lady in this official suburban troupe that gave opéra-comique and vaudeville); St Petersburg, 1831–4 (mistress of the elderly French Ambassador, Marshal Maison, as well as singer in vaudeville); in Paris, at Variétés, 1837, mistress of Heinrich Heine, 1838, trying for Opéra-Comique; Naples, 1839, sang La sonnambula, Teatro del Fondo, failed in Puritani duet at San Carlo;[52]

3 Mlle Olivier, at Opéra-Comique, 1829 (chorus soprano), 1835 (small part); perhaps identifiable as Césarine Olivier, ex-Conservatoire pupil born c. 1803, who sang at Opéra-Comique and St Petersburg, both 1837, Nîmes and Montpellier, 1845–8;

4 Adèle Olivier and perhaps another Mme Olivier who sang in south-
west France (Montpellier, Nîmes, Toulouse, Bordeaux, Bayonne),
1826–37;

5 Mme Olivier and Mme Olivier jeune who sang in north and east France
and Belgium (Namur, Tournai, Nancy, etc.), 1829–37;

6 Phrosine (Euphrosine) Olivier, extra member of chorus at Opéra, 1819,
asked for rise, on being denied it, resigned; second-billed singer in
Théâtre de la Banlieue, second troupe, 1826–9; St Petersburg,
1835–7, 1843–6 (minor parts in vaudevilles; the second conductor
was Alfred Olivier).[53]

The last of these singers, Euphrosine, had a brother and sister
who were both in the corps de ballet of the Opéra. The brother
danced from 1823 to 1829, and in 1831 became an usher (indicateur,
then placeur); he still held the post in 1838. The sister was

7 Honorine Olivier, aged ten in 1819 when Euphrosine got her into the
children's corps de ballet at the Opéra; entered the adult corps, 1
January 1824; withdrawn by her mother, March 1824–March 1825,
because of puberty and rapid growth; on her return, described by
the stage director and the administrator as a good dancer and a 'tall
and beautiful woman'; dismissed, 1828, for an unspecified
misdemeanour, but allowed to return, first temporarily, then
permanently; was still in the corps de ballet when she went on leave
from 2 May to 22 August 1833, and then resigned on 22 October
1833.

Of our seven candidates, no. 1 is too early, the provincial singers
(nos. 4 and 5) are out of the running, nos. 3 and 6, Césarine and
Euphrosine, are possible, but Césarine was probably too old in early
nineteenth-century terms, and Euphrosine was a minor artist,
confined to unfashionable theatres and unlikely to have been in the
right swim. The only ones whose careers and dates fit are no. 2,
Jenny, and no. 7, Honorine.

There is no sure means of identifying one or the other as Mme
Levy. If Jenny were she, Bellini would have had as his hostess (and
perhaps occasional mistress) an experienced woman who a few

years later was living with Heine – after Heine's perfidious treatment of Bellini in his writings, so that need not be put down to jealousy. Hiller, on the other hand, who wrote freely in an 1839 letter of Jenny's affair with the French Ambassador in St Petersburg, said nothing of any connection with Bellini; yet the point of mentioning her was to report her failure in Bellini's music. She came from the strictly French world of opéra-comique and vaudeville, which a few Italian composers (Paër, Carafa) had ventured into. Bellini too ran abortive negotiations with the Opéra-Comique, but the presence of those earlier Italians makes it unnecessary to imagine a link through Mlle Olivier.

Honorine, on the other hand, came from the world of the Opéra, where Rossini and earlier Italians had had great successes; Bellini too had his sights trained on it. Her beauty and her correct spelling – in contrast to the semi-literate writing of her mother and sister – suggest the attributes and training of an apprentice courtesan. The unspecified misdemeanour for which she was to have been dismissed in 1828 tells us nothing (it could, under the stricter Restoration regime, have had to do with sexual conduct, but it could just as well have been the common offence of faking illness and dancing in another theatre). The dates of her leave and resignation in 1833 fit in with Levy's return from Milan about that time or a little earlier, and perhaps with a pregnancy, followed by establishment as his 'wife'. Aymé, meeting her while she was still dancing as Mlle Olivier, would have been sixteen or at most seventeen – just old enough to frequent the green room. She herself was between twenty-four and twenty-six years old in 1834–5. Jenny's age is not known but, given a singing début in 1829, was probably within a year or two of Honorine's.

New evidence may one day bring a clear answer. It matters little. Whether Jenny or Honorine, young Mlle Olivier had, perhaps temporarily, forsaken the theatre for what later came to be known as a sugar daddy.

1 The following is the text of the letter as published in Florimo, B, pp. 107–8:

[7 June 1835]

Dearest Florimo,

　　The premature death of poor Maddalena has broken my heart, and it is easier to grasp than to describe the rending sensation it produced in my spirit: on reading your letter I wept bitterly at her loss. How much of the past came back to mind! how many memories! how many promises! how many hopes!! How transitory everything is in this world of deceptive shows! May God receive her soul into his eternal glory: earth did not deserve to have her: I like very much both of the poems you had written expressly for this mournful circumstance and adorned with the saddest music, and from the tears I shed as I tried to sing them between sobs, I see all too well that my wounded heart is still liable, if not to love, then certainly to suffer . . . Enough!! I don't want to sadden you further: get the author of *Due Speranze* to write a poem for me, in keeping with Maddalena's rare virtues and tender affections, then I'll set it to music, and thus obey with pleasure the person who wishes for a song by me dedicated to her. Arrange for it to be a reply to *Due Speranze*, for it'll then be sure to be tender; and arrange for me to address her beautiful spirit. Farewell, dear Florimo; the pen falls from my hand and tears prevent me from going on. Return the love of

BELLINI.

I wrote this letter yesterday, stunned as I was, and forgot it on my desk; now I am going myself to post it, and I'll add as PS that the fatal news of Maddalena's death, falling like a thunderbolt from heaven (which seems to be angry with me), has thrown a dark pall over my heart, swollen with tears, and has made me sad, dreadfully sad!! For some days now a mournful idea has followed me everywhere and I'm even afraid to tell it you . . . Well!! Here it is, don't take fright. It seems to me, and I tell you this with a shudder,

that in a little while I'll have to follow into the grave the poor girl
who is no more, and whom I once loved so much. May this unlucky
portent be dispelled! Don't say these fears are childish: that's how I
am. What would you? . . . be sorry for me, or mourn for me as best
suits you, my dear Florimo. Farewell!

The following is the authentic text of the letter as published in E,
pp. 560–2. Passages in square brackets indicate damage to the
original or illegible words. Florimo published as a separate letter,
dated 5 June, a version of the first paragraph and of the second half
of the fourth paragraph.

7 June 1835

My duel is an utter fabrication, dear Florimo. I see a few women
but the husbands are against duels on principle – I, as you know,
avoid people of ill repute; so I never expose myself, I don't like
playing Don Juan or Don Quixote, and I therefore hope to die in my
bed as the most peace-loving of men; so when you again get such
news, put it in quarantine before giving it credence. –
    In my last I enclosed the bill for Zingarelli; get him to pay you
at once, as I have already paid. – Here's [   ] for the Duchess of
Noja – Rossini 5 francs: Carafa 5 fcs: Lablache 10 fcs: Rubini 15 fcs:
[   ] 5 fcs; carriage to Marseilles 15 fcs: in all 45 fcs – Here's
your account. Hummel Method 80 fcs: Cramer Etudes 1st and 2nd
part 42 fcs: Weber overtures Euryanthe and Oberon 20 fcs: in all
142: with 60% discount 56.80 net. – The caricature of Rossini is a
gift from me – Ferri's, which Pacini put into the crate, is I think for
Donizetti, so you'll send it on to him. Once and for all let me tell
you that I run errands for you better than others would, and if you
don't want to lose your money you should always make use of me,
if on the other hand you want to act like a Calabrian do as you wish,
I won't interfere – The plaster casts for [the Duchess of] Noja left
Paris over a month ago, if they haven't yet reached Naples what do
you expect me to do about it?
    The news of poor Maddalenina's death afflicted me excessively;
and see how odd it is: [   ] moment I stopped [   ] love [   ]
Giuditta, or rather when I forced myself to forget her, I didn't weep
[   ] not a single tear came into my eyes: Giuditta's conduct had
stopped my heart from giving way; but when I got this sad news,
when I read the poems you set to music, I wept bitterly, and I saw

that my heart was still capable of feeling sorrow: enough, let's
not talk about it. Get the author of the poem *Due Speranze* to write
another for me, in keeping with Maddalenina's virtues and tender
affection, and I'll set it to music, that way I'll obey with pleasure
the person who wishes for a song by me dedicated to her memory:
arrange for it to be a reply to *Due Speranze*; for it'll certainly be
tender, and arrange for me to speak to her beautiful spirit!!

I gave your romanzas to Pacini to be printed: he [   ] me some
copies for our friends in Paris. As you're not known here for your
early compositions there'll be n[   ] to be earned even if Pacini
had the property; but he tells me that the law here gives [   ]
property to the publisher if he brings it out the same day as it's
published by someone else abroad; in a word, I myself see that in
printing them he's doing you and me a favour, because Italian
romanzas by an unknown composer don't sell: if they're sung in
society and strike people as being effective in accordance with
Parisian taste, publishers will ask you for more and will pay for
them – When you come to Paris you yourself will come to
understand this, and you'll see that Cottrau was mistaken in telling
you you could earn well. – Your reply to the Società was fine, and
I'll wait for them to write to me direct: you'll have a copy of my
reply – Tell Cottrau I can't negotiate with publishers, unless for the
sale of the entire property, with the right to sell it to anyone, and
the price of that would be too high for an ordinary publisher – I'd
like the Società to write to me: I intend to ask for 1,800 ducats for
my work and for expenses, to give it the copy adapted for Malibran,
and to charge it from two to three thousand francs for the copy
[   ] it would certainly need for the company it has engaged.
Farewell, dear Florimo.

[?Guardata] has given me two letters for his friends in Naples –
For the moment I'm sending you one of them – The other by a later
post, for it's a whole sheet – I see Don [?Costantino] wants to open
a correspondence with his friends through me: try to avoid it, for I
don't want to pay money on others' behalf; it's all right to enclose
little notes, but letters!!!

Pastura, BSLS, pp. 619–20, pointed out the discrepancy but did not,
as an historian would have done, draw conclusions about Florimo's
evidence as a whole.

2 E, pp. 385–7, gives – without comment – two texts, one originally

published in Antonino Amore's biography (Catania, 1894)
and checked against the autograph in MB, the other originally
published by Florimo in 1882 as a copy sent him by Bellini, and
stated by Cambi to have been checked against the autograph in
the Conservatorio S. Pietro a Majella, Naples. The former is
undoubtedly the original. The Naples 'copy' differs considerably
from it; it also differs in some particulars from Florimo's published
version, which, for instance, adds 'S. Carlo' to identify the 'G[ran]
Teatro' referred to, and makes a thorough muddle by having Bellini
say that the opera he is working on for Paris is due to be staged by
30 May 1835 (whereas, according to both the original and the
'copy', he wrote that he might be able to provide an opera *for Naples*
by that date). That the Naples 'autograph copy' is in fact Florimo's
adapted draft version (which, when he came to publish it, he
titivated further and, at one point, mistranscribed) is exceedingly
likely: why should Bellini send Florimo, who was helping him in
negotiations with the Naples management, a much embellished
version of the letter he was sending that very day to that same
management? Why should he write two lines to Florimo to enclose
a copy when his habit was to enclose copies with a full letter?
Unfortunately the Naples material is not now accessible for
checking. Cambi's action could be explained in various
(speculative) ways, possibly by her having mistakenly set down as
by Bellini her own transcription of a document in Florimo's hand.
It is at all events curious that she did not question the discrepancies
between the original and the 'copy'.

3 Florimo, B, pp. 56 (note), 128–36, made a sustained attempt to
show that Bellini and Donizetti had parallel careers and shared a
'friendship that was kept up, firm and unchangeable, until Bellini's
death'. He related the following episodes, backed by quotations of
what Bellini and Donizetti had supposedly said at the time (Bellini
to Florimo, Donizetti to his Naples friend Teodoro Ghezzi), and by
letters or extracts from them, for none of which is an autograph
known:

a Bellini and Florimo, urged by the *maestrino* Carlo Conti, went to
   Donizetti's *La zingara* in May 1822; Bellini was so enthusiastic
   that he acquired a copy of the score and studied and played it
   'every day, so it never left the music stand of his harpsichord'.

He had himself introduced to Donizetti and came back saying 'Apart from this Lombard's great talent, he is also a very handsome man, and his aspect, noble, benign and at the same time imposing, inspires sympathy and respect' ('These', Florimo adds, 'are his exact words, which I still remember'; the words sound just as stilted in Italian as they do in translation).

b   On the first night of *Adelson e Salvini* in 1825 Donizetti rushed on stage to congratulate Bellini, who was moved to speechless tears and tried to kiss his hand; Donizetti predicted a great future for him.

c   In 1826, when Donizetti was writing *Otto mesi in due ore* for the Nuovo and Bellini *Bianca e Gernando* for the San Carlo, Bellini told Florimo: 'I am really frightened, dear Florimo, of writing an opera in the city where a Donizetti is writing: I so little expert in composing for the theatre, and he whom all Italy deservedly salutes as an outstanding master.' Oddly, it was Donizetti, in an authentic letter, who expressed anxiety about the success of his opera, coming as it would after Bellini's: W. Ashbrook, *The Operas of Donizetti*, Cambridge, 1982, p. 38. (The opera, incidentally, was not *Otto mesi* – first given in 1827 – but *Don Gregorio*, as *L'ajo nell'imbarazzo* was renamed in Naples.)

d   Their Naples successes opened the doors of La Scala to both, and thus sealed their friendship;

e   Bellini and Donizetti were each commissioned to write operas, first for the opening of the Teatro Carlo Felice, Genoa, in 1828, and then for the 1830–1 season at the Teatro Carcano, Milan: 'stimulating each other, as happens in well-born souls', they both achieved equal successes. (Bellini's authentic correspondence shows that he distrusted Donizetti and predicted the failure of his Genoa opera; by the 1830–1 Milan season he saw Donizetti – who had opened first with *Anna Bolena* – as a dangerous rival, all the more because he admired the work, in contrast to much of Donizetti's other output which he ran down as mediocre: Ashbrook, *Operas of Donizetti*, pp. 49–50, E, pp. 536–7.)

f   Donizetti, when someone in Naples denigrated the

orchestration of *La sonnambula* as sounding like a 'French guitar', indignantly contradicted him and praised the work. (The 'guitar' charge was characteristic of late rather than early nineteenth-century comments.)

g   After the first night of *Norma* at La Scala, Donizetti wrote to Ghezzi from Milan that the audience had misjudged it and would change their minds: 'I would be delighted to have composed it and would gladly sign my name to this music.' (Donizetti cannot have been in Milan, as he was then rehearsing a new opera of his own in Naples: Ashbrook, *Operas of Donizetti*, pp. 69–70; H. Weinstock, *Vincenzo Bellini*, New York, 1971, pp. 399–402.)

h   Bellini, in Naples in 1832, on being told that Donizetti had spoken ill of his music, retorted that this was '*impossible, humanly impossible*'; when Florimo suggested it was no more than 'unlikely', he asked 'with that naivety that was the very picture of his beautiful spirit' how Florimo could 'suspect that Donizetti, my friend, whom I so much love and esteem, could speak ill of my music, when I have never spoken ill of his'. (If Bellini had said this, it would have been a lie and Florimo would have known from his earlier letters that it was.)

i   In almost simultaneous operas, *Beatrice di Tenda* and *Parisina*, Bellini and Donizetti used the same theme. When they met, Donizetti mildly brought up Bellini's having lifted the theme from him; Bellini as mildly denied it and said they must both have got it from another source; Donizetti eventually wrote Bellini a two-line letter saying he had found the source in Weber. Florimo claims to have related this episode 'exactly as Bellini wrote it to me in one of his letters'. (As *Parisina* had its first performance in Florence one day after that of *Beatrice* in Venice, Donizetti could scarcely have thought Bellini had lifted from it.)

j   When Bellini and Donizetti both composed for the Paris Théâtre-Italien in 1835, Donizetti wrote to Felice Romani 'I do not deserve the triumph of *I puritani*', but his *Marino Faliero* was a triumph too. (Bellini's letters at the time show his jealousy and distrust and his conviction that *Marino* was a failure.) This 'letter' first appeared in A. Pougin, *Bellini*, Paris, 1868, which also printed the 'letter' about the 'fiasco!!! fiasco!!! fiasco!!!' of *Norma*, supplied by Florimo.

k Donizetti, preparing to compose *Lucia di Lammermoor* in Naples after Bellini's death, felt challenged when a friend said it was a pity Bellini had died, as *Lucia* would have been just the subject for him. After its triumph, Donizetti met the friend and asked 'Have I done wrong to my friend Bellini? . . . On the contrary, I invoked his beautiful spirit, and it inspired me to write *Lucia*.' (*Lucia* had its first night on 26 September 1835; news of Bellini's death three days earlier did not reach Naples until 8 October: BSLS, p. 536.)

4 In a highly suspect 'letter', paraphrased in 1839 by a Sicilian writer (for which no autograph has ever been seen), Bellini allegedly expressed his intention of setting Alfieri's tragedy *Oreste* word for word, on the principles followed by the later Wagner and Richard Strauss, though Florimo denied that he had ever mentioned it. Fragments setting the classical stories of Virginia and Iphigenia (among Bellini's papers in MB) have generally been taken to be student exercises. M. R. Adamo, 'Vincenzo Bellini. Biografia', in Adamo and F. Lippmann, *Vincenzo Bellini*, Turin, 1981, pp. 190–1, argues that the Alfieri project is 'absolutely plausible', because of 'Bellini's passion for Alfieri, and his conception of opera [as shown in *Norma*]', and that the college exercises 'may indicate that he was not so unwilling to attempt "classical" subjects'. 'Bellini's passion for Alfieri', however, is attested only by Florimo's statement; that he once described his preferred librettist Romani as 'my Alfieri' (E, p. 445) tells us little. He certainly dismissed the subject of Caesar in Egypt as 'old as Noah' (E, p. 177) and probably made a distinction between classical antiquity (quarried for numberless eighteenth-century operas) and exciting 'new' subjects such as the Gaulish *Norma* – classical though his treatment of it may be in an aesthetic sense. If the classical subjects of his sketches were set by Bellini's teachers they show nothing about his tastes. Cf. the virtual dismissal of the *Oreste* story in Weinstock, *Bellini*, pp. 418–21.

5 The first version of *Adelson e Salvini* was in three acts (a decidedly out of date arrangement at the time), the second version in two; the orchestration of the two versions differs. Neither has come down to

us complete, though there is a printed vocal score of the revised
version, which in turn does not quite correspond to the MS sections
of the revised full score. See S. E. Failla, 'Adelson e Salvini, prima
versione', in *I teatri di Vincenzo Bellini*, Catania, 1986, pp. 15–28; F.
Lippmann, 'Vincenzo Bellini e l'opera seria del suo tempo', in
Adamo and Lippmann, *Vincenzo Bellini*, pp. 446–51, 525–30.

6 The solo instrument introducing 'Sorgi, o padre' was originally a
clarinet, replaced in 1828 by a flute, with flute and clarinet taking
up the aria melody in place of the original cor anglais. The main
new material in 1828 is in Bianca's part (Act 1 cavatina, and final
scena and aria in Act 2). The allegro of the cavatina and a new
chorus later went into *Norma*: more details in Lippmann, in
Adamo and Lippmann, *Vincenzo Bellini*, pp. 452–5, 530–2.

7 Understanding of Romani is much advanced by Alessandro
Roccatagliati's doctoral thesis 'Felice Romani librettista',
University of Bologna, 1993. His findings suggest that Romani's
widow Emilia Branca, in her *Felice Romani e i più reputati maestri di
musica del suo tempo*, Turin, 1882, was more accurate on matters of
fact than has sometimes been alleged, though she inflated her
husband's role in the careers of Bellini, Donizetti, and others. See
also S. Maguire, *Vincenzo Bellini and the Aesthetics of Early Nineteenth-
Century Italian Opera*, New York and London, 1989; M. Mauceri,
'Inediti di Felice Romani. La carriera del librettista attraverso nuovi
documenti dagli archivi milanesi', *Nuova Rivista Musicale Italiana*,
July–December 1992, pp. 391–432.

8 Pacini's claim, in a statement to an early biographer and in his own
unreliable *Memorie artistiche*, Florence, 1875, that he befriended and
helped Bellini does not fit the facts: BSLS, pp. 90–2, 297–300.

9 Bellini to Giuditta Pasta, September 1831, in F. Lippmann, ed.,
'Belliniana', in *Il melodramma italiano dell'Ottocento. Studi e ricerche
per Massimo Mila*, Turin, 1977, pp. 281–317, p. 284; to Florimo,
13 October 1834, E, p. 460.

10 E, pp. 397, 432–3.

11 Bellini to Ferdinando Artaria, 22 January 1830, in L. Cambi, ed.,
'Bellini. Un pacchetto di autografi', in *Scritti in onore di Luigi Ronga*,
Milan-Naples, 1973, pp. 53–90, pp. 64–6. Cambi suggests a
personal motive – a Mme Artaria was housekeeper in the Turina
household. It seems much more likely that Bellini's motive was,

as he stated, a professional one. He had a connection with Artaria, who was to publish the separate numbers from *Capuleti*, while Ricordi had the rights in the score.

12 Giovanni Ricordi to Nicola Vaccai, 6 October, 6 November 1826, Archivio Vaccai, Biblioteca Comunale, Tolentino (he asked the reluctant Vaccai to send him from Trieste the score or parts of Mercadante's *Donna Caritea*, then new); G. Cottrau, *Lettres d'un mélomane*, Naples, 1885, p. 77; [Carlo Conti] to Marchese Bartolomeo Capranica, 22 November 1827, Biblioteca Teatrale del Burcardo, Rome, Fondo Capranica (offering a copy of *Maometto II* much cheaper than the impresario Barbaja would charge for a legitimate copy); G. Vaccai, *Vita di Nicola Vaccai*, Bologna, 1882, p. 136 (for London). The Paris impresarios who put on *Puritani*, Edouard Robert and Carlo Severini, had earlier tried to buy cheap pirated scores of *Straniera* and *Capuleti*: to the agent Buttazzoni, 21 June 1832, AN Paris AJ13 1161/IV.

13 When Bellini composed *La sonnambula* he could not have heard *Guillaume Tell*, which was not performed in Italy until some months later, but he could easily have read a vocal score. It is also conceivable that Alessandro Lanari, impresario of *Capuleti* (carnival 1830), *Tell* (autumn 1831), and – in partnership with Giuseppe Crivelli and Bartolomeo Merelli – *Norma* (carnival 1832), let him see the full score. The *ranz des vaches* was in any case a folk tune.

14 The latter three chords were written in after the autograph score had gone into rehearsal, to establish a new key of D flat into which, to accommodate the singers, the succeeding recitative and duet had had to be transposed down from the original E flat: F. Degrada, 'Prolegomeni a una lettura della *Sonnambula*', in *Il melodramma italiano dell'Ottocento*, pp. 319–50, pp. 344–5. This may be considered a happy accident.

15 There is probably also an influence from the ensembles in Spontini's *La vestale*, well known in Naples when Bellini was studying there. The parallel sometimes drawn with the nobility of Gluck's reform operas is perhaps in the minds of later hearers rather than in Bellini's, though *Iphigénie en Aulide* had been put on at the San Carlo, Naples, in 1812 and he might have seen a score in the Conservatorio library.

16 A discarded version of the cabaletta to 'Casta diva' has Norma

express guilt at having to 'defend a perfidious people who give us chains by way of peace'. Romani's widow maintained that this had been forbidden by the censorship. It may have been – 'chains', like 'liberty', was a trigger word for censors – but the words may have been rejected by Bellini on metrical/musical grounds. The libretto passed by the censor still has plenty of fighting talk about Gaulish revolt. For the tangled problem of the various versions, see Roccatagliati, 'Felice Romani', p. 84.

17 Pastura in BSLS, pp. 285, 345 (followed by Weinstock, *Bellini*, p. 494, and by Adamo, *Bellini*, p. 186) muddled the circumstances of this contract. Early in 1830 Bellini signed with Giuseppe Crivelli (then impresario of La Scala and La Fenice in partnership with Alessandro Lanari) a contract for two operas for autumn 1831 and carnival 1832. This contract was bought out by the management that commissioned *La sonnambula* at the Teatro Carcano, Milan, in carnival 1831. Bellini then made a fresh contract with the Crivelli-Lanari management (now joined by Bartolomeo Merelli) for *Norma*, put on by Merelli alone ten days after Crivelli's death on 16 December 1831: E, pp. 299–300; Merelli to Lanari, 17 December 1831, Biblioteca Nazionale, Florence, Carteggi Vari 396/8. Pastura thought Bellini was still bound in 1832 by the 1830 contract and, after *Norma*, had one opera to work off (he was perhaps misled by Bellini's reference in a letter to Ricordi of 16 September 1832, E, p. 322, to a contractual relationship with the Crivelli heirs; this presumably concerned secondary rights in *Norma*). If he had been so bound, Bellini would not have been able to earn over 10,000 francs for *Norma* – instead of the 8,700 provided for in the 1830 contract – or to bargain as he did with Lanari for a similar fee for Venice in carnival 1833.

18 Lanari's troubles in the run-up to the 1833 carnival season are documented in Fondazione Levi, Venice, Archivio del Teatro La Fenice, Processi verbali convocazioni, b. 5, Spettacoli, b. 3. He had to compensate the owners by giving fifty-six instead of fifty performances, and four operas instead of three, for an unchanged subsidy. The only compensation he got from Pasta for her insistence on keeping prices unchanged was her agreeing to sing thirty-five expensive performances instead of the stipulated forty. Lanari's disgust at the uncooperative conduct of the theatre owners

led him in effect to throw up the management after the end of the season.

19 In a suspect letter of 24 August 1832, published (and probably embellished) by Florimo, B, pp. 400–2, Bellini expresses astonishment that *Norma* should have been such a success in Bergamo, the home town of Donizetti and his teacher Mayr. *La straniera* had been a success there in 1830, so he had no reason to be apprehensive. An authentic letter to Count Barbò, 23 August 1832, E, pp. 318–19, expresses straightforward delight.

20 A somewhat suspect letter to Filippo Santocanale, dated 17 February 1833, and published by Florimo, B, pp. 405–6, for which no autograph has been seen, has Bellini despairing of finishing the opera on time and foreseeing a flop. The rest of the letter seems genuine enough, but this forecast may be one of Florimo's neat dramatic points. Bellini's other letters give the impression that he was disinclined either to forecast or to acknowledge a total flop.

21 Bellini to Ricordi, 12 November 1833, catalogue of Sotheby's sale of Continental manuscripts and music, 26 May 1994. He complained that he had not been informed in London of the Milan production, which would have given him an opportunity. A similar letter of 21 March to the composer Giuseppe Bornaccini, but including the words 'solenne fiasco', may have been embellished by Florimo, who published it in B, pp. 344–5.

22 Bellini wrote 'accatterà', literally 'he will beg from [or 'wheedle'] me no more': to Ricordi, 6 January 1833, catalogue of Sotheby's sale of Continental printed books, manuscripts, and music, 2 December 1993.

23 Bellini to Romani, draft, E, pp. 412–13. This is the text originally published, with other, fragmentary drafts, by A. Amore in 1892. A longer text was published by R. Barbiera, *Grandi e piccole memorie*, Florence, 1910, p. 484, with the date 29 May 1834: BSLS, pp. 375–7, where it is assumed to be the 'definitive version'. It is obviously worked up from the draft, but with those embellishments and added fulsome compliments to Romani that – we now know – mark Florimo's versions of Bellini's letters to his librettist. It may indeed have come from Florimo, who supplied at least one other writer with a 'letter' to Romani. Barbiera himself was not the most

reliable of editors. It is safer to stick to the draft, though it too
now lacks a verifiable autograph.

24 Bellini to Romani, 7 October 1834, extracts in catalogue of
Sotheby's sale of Continental manuscripts and music, 21 November
1990 (the text in E, pp. 447–8, is seriously corrupt: see p. 9); 4
January 1835, in F. Walker, ed., 'Lettere disperse e inedite di
Vincenzo Bellini', *Rivista del Comune di Catania*, October–December
1966, p. 13.

25 Turina's letters to Florimo (plus one from her close friend
Countess Virginia Martini), between January 1834 and February
1836, give her version of these and later developments: F. Walker,
'Giuditta Turina and Bellini', *Music and Letters* 70, 1959, pp. 19–34;
BSLS, pp. 664–87, 693–706.

26 Bellini to Giuditta Pasta, 26 August 1833, in Lippmann,
'Belliniana', p. 287.

27 *Morning Chronicle*, 2 May, 24 June, 8 August 1833; *Morning Herald*,
24 June 1833. A favourable notice did appear in the *Morning Post*
(translation, E, pp. 373–4), but it was a puff for Pasta and said
nothing about *Norma* as an opera. A favourable notice attributed
to *The Times* in the contemporary Milan *Eco*, and mentioned in a
suspect letter of Bellini published by a Sicilian author (ibid.
pp. 374–5), does not appear in the microfilm file of that newspaper;
it may have appeared elsewhere. See E. J. Dent, 'Bellini in
Inghilterra', in I. Pizzetti, ed., *Bellini*, Milan, 1940, pp. 155–83; J.
Budden, 'La fortuna di Bellini in Inghilterra', in *Atti del convegno
internazionale di studi belliniani*, Catania, 1985, pp. 225–31.

28 The extent of Rossini's influence on the score of *Puritani* is not
known. It is almost certainly untrue that (as Florimo asserted)
Bellini submitted the entire score for Rossini's judgment with a
humble covering letter offering to let him 'cut, add to, or modify
the whole thing, if you think fit, and it will benefit my music'. This
passage was supposedly 'literally transcribed' from a 'letter' of
Bellini to Florimo of 14 December 1834, which Florimo did not
otherwise publish and which has never been seen. He also published
an 'extract' from a 'letter' dated 15 May 1833 comparing *Guillaume
Tell* (which, Bellini is made to say, he had heard thirty times) to
Dante's *Divine Comedy*: Florimo, B, pp. 51–4. At the supposed date,

Bellini could not have heard *Tell* even three times. This seems to
be another of Florimo's attempts to establish both Bellini's virtues
and his harmonious relations with fellow-composers.

29 For the complex story of the various versions, of which only a
summary is given here, G. Pugliese and R. Vlad, eds., *I Puritani
ritrovati*, Manduria, 1986, and Lippmann, *Vincenzo Bellini*, pp. 544–8.
The Naples version, to fit the company available, turned Riccardo
from a baritone into a tenor. Its score, though long since known,
was not performed or published till the 1980s. Bellini in the end left
out 'Suoni la tromba' as politically impossible, but sent it along
anyhow as a separate, untransposed piece. It was in fact performed
(in the Paris version) throughout the despotic Italian states by the
simple expedient of changing 'libertà' to 'lealtà' ('loyalty') and
'patria' to 'gloria'. In Paris the police had twice reminded the
Théâtre-Italien management about the regulation setting an 11
p.m. curtain time: Préfet de Police to Robert, 26 November 1831,
20 February 1834, AN Paris AJ¹³ 1161.

30 This 'letter' was published by Florimo, B, pp. 482–4, as a fragment
headed 'Paris, undated (1834)'. It is suspect because (a) Bellini
generally dated his letters to Florimo; (b) it contains matter (about
Puritani and his negotiations with the Opéra) that could have been
written only some time after the end of January 1835; (c) it states
that Romani had written to Bellini commenting on the *Puritani*
libretto, whereas there is no sign that Bellini received any letter
from Romani between 4 October 1834 (when the libretto was not
yet available) and April 1835, at which time he was still awaiting a
reply to his letter to Romani of 4 January; (d) most important, the
part of the letter dealing with marriage plans duplicates and
coarsens some of the content of Bellini's authentic letter to Florimo
of 30 November 1834. It looks as though, at the very least, Florimo
took parts of more than one Bellini letter to concoct this one,
rephrased them, and added matter of his own. His motive is
unclear. Bellini's dealings with women perhaps stirred his
imagination.

31 Original extracts and covering letter of 13 February 1880, MB,
extracts (unaltered) and letter (slightly altered, and undated)
printed in Florimo, B, pp. 61–3. – This appendix follows on my
article 'Vita e morte di Bellini a Parigi', *Rivista Italiana di Musicologia*

19, 1984, pp. 261–76, since which I have been able to do more nearly exhaustive research; this has led me to new information and in part different conclusions.

32 F. Pastura, ed., *Le lettere di Bellini*, Catania, 1935, p. 178.

33 All information about Aymé's diplomatic career is based on his file in Archives du Ministère des Affaires Etrangères, Paris, Agents, Personnel série I, vol. XII.

34 C. d'Hozier and M. Bachelin-Deflorenne, *Etat présent de la noblesse française*, 5th edn, Paris, 1884.

35 AN Paris AJ^{13} 462/I. For the foyer de la danse, L. Véron, *Mémoires d'un bourgeois de Paris*, Paris, 1853–5, III, ch. 5.

36 S. Levy to Rosario Bellini, 15 December 1835, MB, published in BSLS, pp. 539–40 (which however fails to reproduce Levy's mistakes in French and Italian: he wrote 'Capucins' for 'Capucines' and 'la sua mallatia è stato' for 'la sua malattia è stata').

37 B. Condorelli, *Il Museo Belliniano*, Catania, 1935.

38 Bellini to Ponzani, 30 May 1835, E, pp. 558–9; Ponzani to Bellini, 11, 18 June, 28 July 1835, in BSLS, pp. 480–1, 487, 504.

39 Adopted for example by David Levy for the Liverpool department store he founded, Lewis's, and by the noted criminal lawyer J. G. Lewis (whose family were originally Loew).

40 E, p. 283.

41 Bellini to Ponzani (see note 38).

42 Description of flats at this address in 1852 municipal survey, Archives de la Ville, Paris, DP4.

43 E, p. 500.

44 E, pp. 422, 444, 541, 602; Rosario Bellini to Rossini, 26 October 1835, 14 February 1836, MB.

45 What follows is based on a search through manuscript genealogies in the Lucien Wolf papers, Mocatta Library, University College, London, and the many genealogies and Jewish pedigrees in the Colyer-Fergusson and Hyamson collections, at the Society of Genealogists, London, as well as in London probate records, the published *Bevis Marks Records*, *London Post Office Directories* from 1808 to 1887, *City of London Pollbook*, 1836, *Pigot's London and Provincial Commercial Directories*, 1826–7 and 1832–3–4, and *City of London Directory*, 1879.

46 A Jewish marriage is recorded in the Colyer-Fergusson collection

between Eugène Picard, of Geneva, and Jeannette, daughter of
Laurence Levy (19 January 1859). This appears to be a separate
Picard-Levy connection.

47 *Pigot's London and Provincial Commercial Directory*, 1832–3–4, lists at
Stoke Newington, among 'gentry and clergy', a Mr Lewis, but the
1874 *Post Office Directory of the Six Home Counties* shows, at the same
address, a James Dudley Lewis, presumably a gentile. The
1832–3–4 directory listed a Rothschild but no Levy. Perhaps a
wholesale slopseller's younger brother did not qualify as gentry.

48 An entry in the Jewish pedigrees at the Society of Genealogists
(JD9.23) has a Solomon Levy, born 1785, married to Arabella
Joseph (daughter of Lyon Joseph), died Bristol, 1841, without
further details. Jewish surnames were few, so this may be a
different couple.

49 Giuditta Turina to Francesco Florimo, 18 January 1836, BSLS, pp.
703–4. The writer and political exile Niccolò Tommaseo described
Mme Levy as Levy's 'wife or mistress [*amica*]', adding that Bellini
was her lover [*amico*], but as he also passed on false rumours this
evidence has less weight: to Gino Capponi, 12/15 October 1835,
in Tommaseo and Capponi, *Carteggio inedito*, eds. I. Del Lungo and
P. Prunas, Bologna, 1911–32, I, pp. 312–15.

50 Véron, *Mémoires d'un bourgeois de Paris*, III, ch. 5.

51 The archives of the Opéra in AN AJ¹³ and in the Bibliothèque de
l'Opéra, Paris, and the *Almanach des spectacles parisiens*, are the main
sources; also the Paris *Gazette des théâtres* and *Courrier des théâtres*, and
H. Lyonnet, ed., *Dictionnaire des comédiens français*, Geneva, [c. 1912].

52 For her St Petersburg and Naples activities: *Aus Ferdinand Hillers
Briefwechsel (1826–1861)*, ed. R. Seitz, Cologne, Festgabe zum 7.
Kongress der internationalen Gesellschaft für Musikwissenschaft,
1958, p. 37; for her affair with Heine, G. Meyerbeer, *Briefwechsel und
Tagebücher*, ed. H. and G. Becker, Berlin, 1960–, III, p. 675.

53 Documentation on Euphrosine Olivier in AN Paris AJ¹³ 128, on her
brother and her sister Honorine (see below) in AJ¹³ 116/III, 120/II,
121, and in Bibliothèque de l'Opéra PE3, PE26.

The chief sources for Bellini's life are his letters. The Introduction sets out the difficulties of using them. Fresh Bellini letters turn up from time to time at auction, and sometimes show the published text to be corrupt.

The fundamental collection (which also quotes many contemporary reviews of the operas) is V. Bellini, *Epistolario*, ed. L. Cambi, Milan, 1943. Cambi was a careful editor who realized that some texts were suspect, but she did not go beyond leaving out the most outrageous fakes. Other letters appeared in F. Pastura, *Bellini secondo la storia*, Parma, 1959, a massive biography that likewise exploded the more grotesque legends without taking a clear stand on the remaining dubious material; Pastura's transcriptions are not always quite accurate. Smaller groups of letters in F. Walker, ed., 'Giuditta Turina and Bellini', *Music and Letters* 40, 1959, pp. 19–34, and 'Lettere disperse e inedite di Vincenzo Bellini', *Rivista del Comune di Catania* 8, 1960, pp. 106–18; L. Cambi, ed., 'Un pacchetto di autografi', in *Studi in onore di Luigi Ronga*, Milan, 1973, pp. 53–90; F. Lippmann, ed., 'Belliniana', in *Il melodramma italiano dell'Ottocento. Studi e ricerche per Massimo Mila*, Turin, 1977. All of these (but no new ones) are grouped in C. Neri, ed., *Le lettere di Bellini*, Catania, 1993, with a (not always judicious) commentary.

Besides Pastura's, the chief modern biographies (commented on in the body of this book) are by H. Weinstock, *Vincenzo Bellini. His Life and his Operas*, New York/London, 1971/2, M. R. Adamo, 'Vincenzo Bellini. Biografia', in Adamo and Lippmann, *Vincenzo Bellini*, Turin, 1981, and G. Tintori, *Bellini*, Milan, 1983. An important survey of all that is known of Bellini's early years is S. E. Failla, *Bellini Vincenzo in Catania*, Catania, 1985.

The leading critical study of the music is F. Lippmann, 'Vincenzo Bellini e l'opera seria del suo tempo', in Adamo and Lippmann, *Vincenzo Bellini* (a revised version of a study first published in German in *Analecta Musicologica* 6, 1969); there is a deeply knowledgeable survey of Italian opera practice in Bellini's day by J. Budden, *The Operas of Verdi*, London, 1973–81, I, ch. 1, and a more skittish one by E. J. Dent, *The Rise of Romantic Opera*, ed. W. Dean, Cambridge, 1976. The volume by L. Orrey in the Master Musicians series, London, 1969, is still useful. Notable studies of individual operas are F. Degrada, 'Prolegomeni ad una lettura della *Sonnambula*', in *Il melodramma italiano dell'Ottocento*, and P. Petrobelli's two studies of *I puritani*, in his *Music in the Theater*, Princeton, 1994. D. Kimbell, *Italian Opera*, Cambridge, 1991, deals sensitively with Bellini's music and with *Norma* in particular. A. Einstein, 'Vincenzo Bellini', *Music and Letters* 16, 1935, pp. 325–32, is characteristically pithy. The 150th anniversary in 1985 brought a number of very uneven publications, chief among them *Atti del convegno internazionale di studi belliniani*, Catania, 1985.

On Bellini's treatment of words and his dealings with his librettist Romani, S. Maguire, *Vincenzo Bellini and the Aesthetics of Early Nineteenth-Century Opera*, New York/London, 1989, is complemented by the important Bologna doctoral thesis of A. Roccatagliati, 'Felice Romani librettista', 1993; one hopes that this will soon be published.

The general background of the Italian opera business and musical world is dealt with by me in *The Opera Industry in Italy from Cimarosa to Verdi. The Role of the Impresario*, Cambridge, 1984, *Music and Musicians in Nineteenth-Century Italy*, London, 1991, and *Singers of Italian Opera: the History of a Profession*, Cambridge, 1992.

The best documents on Bellini are his operas. No attempt is made here at a full discography, because many recordings are of live performances, and of these many are hard to find or of exceedingly poor sound quality.

Most of the leading recordings of *Norma*, *Puritani*, and *Sonnambula* now current have either Maria Callas in the lead (with Tullio Serafin conducting the first two, and Antonino Votto the last) or Joan Sutherland (with Richard Bonynge conducting). The choice is not clear-cut: Callas is incomparably musical and expressive, Sutherland has matchless beauty of voice; Serafin has a profound understanding of the music – with tempi, buoyancy, and use of rubato unobtrusively right – and Votto is not far behind, but Bonynge uses fuller and more up-to-date texts, and the sound quality of his recordings is more modern. The tenors in both series, with one or two exceptions, are badly out of style, however fine their voices.

A tenor who is in style, Alfredo Kraus, sings in a *Puritani* conducted by Riccardo Muti that has a number of virtues but seems wilful in its tempi. For *Beatrice di Tenda* the live-performance recording conducted by Vittorio Gui, with Leyla Gencer (Melodram), seems more idiomatic than the Sutherland/Bonynge studio recording – in spite of Gui's eccentric omission of the final cabaletta.

These seem to be the best recordings of the early operas:

Adelson e Salvini (first version): cond. Failla (Bongiovanni)

Bianca e Fernando: cond. Licata (Nuova Era)

Capuleti: either Baker/Sills, cond. Patanè, or Baltsa/Gruberová, cond. Muti.

Il pirata: Caballé/Labò/Cappuccilli, cond. Capuana (Memories) (preferable to the Caballé/Martí studio recording)

La straniera: Scotto, cond. Sanzogno (Melodram)

Zaira: Ricciarelli, cond. Olmi (Nuova Era)

INDEX

Note: to avoid duplication, the index has no entry for Vincenzo Bellini. His relationships and aspects of his life and career are dealt with under individual and subject entries. Each of his operas has an entry; works by others are entered under their composers or authors.